SELECTIVE BIBLIOGRAPHY
for the Study of
English and American
Literature

SIXTH EDITION

RICHARD D. ALTICK
The Ohio State University
and
ANDREW WRIGHT
University of California, San Diego

Macmillan Publishing Co., Inc.
NEW YORK

Collier Macmillan Publishers
LONDON

Earlier editions © 1960 and 1963, copyright © 1967, 1971, and 1975 by Macmillan Publishing Co., Inc.

Macmillan Publishing Co., Inc.
866 Third Avenue, New York, New York 10022

Collier Macmillan Canada, Ltd.

Library of Congress Cataloging in Publication Data
Altick, Richard Daniel (date)
  Selective bibliography for the study of English and American literature.

  Includes index.
  1. English literature—History and criticism—Bibliography. 2. Bibliography—Bibliography—English literature. 3. American literature—History and criticism—Bibliography. 4. Bibliography—Bibliography—American Literature. 5. Literary research—Handbooks, manuals, etc. 1. Wright, Andrew H., joint author. II. Title.
Z2011.A1A47 1979   [PR83]   016.82   78–4130
ISBN 0–02–302110–1

Printing: 1 2 3 4 5 6 7 8   Year: 9 0 1 2 3 4 5

Selective Bibliography
for the Study of
English and American Literature

Foreword to the Sixth Edition

In the four years since the fifth edition of this book went to press, so many bibliographies and other works important to literary research have been published that another revision has become necessary. Of the approximately 636 numbered items, seventy-two are new and seventy-six have been altered to take account of new editions, supplementary volumes, and the like. Eleven entries found in earlier editions have been omitted from this one because the books that they record have been superseded or, in our opinion, are no longer of primary importance to the student.

Another freshly revised edition may be expected within a few years. Meanwhile we shall, as always, welcome suggestions looking to the increased usefulness of this book.

We are grateful to Kevin O'Connor and Philip Smith for their help in putting the sixth edition together.

R. D. A.
A. W.

Preface

The chief purpose of this compilation is to provide students of English and American literature with a convenient and reasonably authoritative guide to research materials. It is highly selective; many items that have appeared in similar handbooks have been rejected as obsolete, or untrustworthy, or simply not valuable enough for the student to bother with. We have tried always to keep in mind the needs of today's scholars, which in some ways are different from the needs of preceding generations. Thus, the interests and approaches of practicing scholars seem no longer to justify including a "classic" work like Petzholdt's *Bibliotheca Bibliographica* (published in 1866) among the bibliographies every student should know. Accordingly, we have sought to include only those bibliographies and reference works actually used—and usable—by modern scholars. Desire for conciseness has required the omission of many items that have potential usefulness at some point in a given course of investigation, but these can easily be found through the more comprehensive guides that we do include. On the other hand, we have had to list a certain number of inferior works; these cover, however sparsely, ground that would otherwise remain bare. The principle underlying our selection has always been that of Roger Williams, in *A Key into the Language of America* (1643): "A Little *Key* may open a *Box*, where lies a *bunch of Keyes.*" The following pages contain most of the all-important "little" keys.

In addition to listing the books that are indispensable to any program of independent research, whether for a graduate seminar report, a dissertation, or a post-doctoral project, we have had several other purposes in mind. One is to offer a list—again, highly selective—of histories of English and American literature, both general and specialized (that is, confined to specific periods or types). The climate of academic opinion in late years has been somewhat unfavorable to the use of such books by graduate students. But because leisure for the reading of the actual texts of all literary masterpieces is available only in some timeless Utopia, and, on the other hand, the general examination that is the gateway to candidacy for the Ph.D. may range over a thousand years of literary history, a judicious, discriminating use of books like Baugh and Spiller would seem to be not only legitimate but unavoidable. Books *about* literature can be grossly misused by the slothful and the unscrupulous; but so can telephone directories, whose usefulness and legality remain unimpaired by their occasional services to people needing bookmakers. The titles listed here happen to be those that we consider the best in their various fields. When the best is excellent, we have generally allowed no remark of ours, beyond what may be inferred from the inclusion of the book, to distract the reader; when the best is none too good, we have sometimes felt obliged to comment on the book's shortcomings.

Another concern has been to suggest works useful for occasional, incidental reference—to supply biographical data, the details of a Greek myth, the essential information about existentialism, and so on. Here, as elsewhere, we have sought to enable the student to become his own reference librarian, thus releasing those hard-working professional servants of the public for more esoteric pursuits. Every scholar worthy of the name, no matter how many years separate him from the Ph.D. in one direction or the other, must develop to a high degree the all-essential qualities of independence and ingenuity. He should know his way around the bailiwick of miscellaneous bibliography so well that only seldom should he have to enlist the aid of a librarian. Hence this compilation is designed to help him find the answers to many kinds of "reference" questions.

Recognizing as we do that literary studies in recent years have tended to spill into other causeways, we have included a certain number of indispensable items in fields that are not primarily literary. We have, for instance, listed the most important aids to historical and biographical research. Similarly there are sections on social and intellectual history. There is also a list of works which, while they resist classification, are of great importance to any student of literature. Such books as John Livingston Lowes's *The Road to Xanadu,* and Erich Auerbach's *Mimesis* and Henry Nash Smith's *Virgin Land* appear in a separate section that we have called "Some Books Every Student of Literature Should Read."

Altogether, we have attempted to construct a well-rounded *vade mecum* to literary studies, in which every area of concern to the graduate student and the mature scholar has been, at least in some measure, treated.

Believing that in a book of this sort the arrangement should be determined by common sense rather than a pedantic passion for universal consistency, we have let the internal logic of each section decide the order of the entries. Thus the histories of literature appear, within the various subcategories, in order of first publication; but in the sections on cultural and intellectual history and on retrospective national bibliographies, for example, the arrangement, after the listing of general works, is by specific periods covered. A third kind of arrangement appears in the section on American libraries. Here the order is geographical, beginning in New England and progressing westward. In brief, our aim has been to arrange the items as usefully as possible and to make clear, by our choice of ordering, the relationship the various items in each category bear to one another.

In the main body of the book the items are numbered. We have omitted four or five numbers after each section and subsection so that new titles can conveniently be inserted. For edited works, the form of our entry has been determined by the way the work is usually referred to, whether by title or by editor's name. Authors' names are regularly given as they appear on title pages. Subtitles are omitted unless they say something useful. Occasionally, where knowledge of the age of a book is of special pertinence, we have indicated the date of its first publication as well as that of the newest edition. Only one place of publication is given for each title. Thus in style as in arrangement we have tried to be sufficiently detailed, but in such a way as to be desirably short-winded.

R. D. A.
A. W.

Contents

On the Use of Scholarly Tools

No bibliography, indeed no work of reference, is perfect; but some are less perfect than others. All the books listed here are useful in one kind of research or another, and some are absolutely indispensable in their various areas of interest. But to use them undiscriminatingly, without clear understanding of what they have and what they do not have, where they excel and where they fall short, is to waste hours and weeks of precious time.

Before using any reference tool, the student should carefully examine it, to discover not only its avowed but also its unacknowledged strengths, weaknesses, and peculiarities. He should keep in mind the possibility that he will have to refer to the book scores of times in the years to come. His examination should therefore be careful enough to be permanently useful. The time he spends in such a preliminary survey is nearly always repaid, many times over, in the efficiency with which he can then use the book, in the elimination of wasted time (looking for material that simply isn't there), and in the avoidance of the booby trap of erroneous or incomplete information. The following pages are designed to suggest some of the things the student should keep in mind as he encounters a research tool for the first time. The advice is, of course, not exhaustive. But it at least implies the spirit—a mingling of respect and skepticism—in which all such first meetings should be managed.

1. *The front matter.* What are the stated purposes and stated limits of the work? These can seldom be compressed into the few words of a subtitle; they must be explained in detail in a preface or introduction. A single sentence may quickly reveal that the book does not contain the kind of material for which one is looking. Without reading the introduction, it is impossible to know that Besterman's *World Bibliography of Bibliographies* (**502**) * excludes

---

* The bold-face figures in parentheses refer to the numbered items in the main body of this book.

1

a large class of bibliographies: those which were included in larger works but were never issued separately.   But not all introductions are candid and accurate in their description of a book's scope and achievement.   Some, like the magnificently florid overture to Allibone's *Critical Dictionary of English Literature* (**39**)—a work which is the very reverse of critical as we now understand the term—, are nothing more than unblushing blurbs; others, perhaps more modest in tone, are nevertheless only statements of pious intent.   That is why it is always necessary to check up on the promises found in the front matter by actually testing the work and consulting expert opinion.   Many reference works are not what they seem or pretend or would like to be.

In a multi-volume work, published over a considerable period of time, the later volumes may have separate introductions which announce important shifts in policy and scope.   In the course of publication Courtney's *Register of National Bibliography* (**503**) ceased to be "national" and began to include non-British items. Sabin's *Bibliotheca Americana* (**821**) underwent successive contractions of coverage in the later stages of compilation, and one should never use a given volume without first consulting the introduction in Volume XXIX to discover what limitations were in effect at that particular point.   Occasionally, the introductory matter indispensable for efficient use of a work may not appear in the place where one would expect to find it.   In Sir Walter Greg's *Bibliography of the English Printed Drama* (**412**), for instance, it is found in Volume IV.

2. *The book's age.*   Is it of recent origin, according to the date of publication?   The year on the title page may be misleading, for it may merely represent the date of a fresh printing without change of content.   Furthermore, was the book really up-to-date when published?   Some scholarly books may await publication for years, and during the interval between completion and publication the fatigued author may neglect to add recent materials to his manuscript. It has been remarked, truly, that every bibliography is out of date before it is published—the present one doubtless is no exception—but it is desirable to know *how* dated every book really is.

As a very general rule, it is true that a newer book is preferable to an older one; but there are so many exceptions and qualifications that one must examine each case on its own merits.   The newer book published in 1978 may indisputably have the benefit of thirty more years' research than an older one dated 1948, but it may also be less detailed and less reliable. Thus sometimes the work that is superficially "obsolete" may prove by far the more fruitful source to consult. Even books as old as Watt's *Bibliotheca Britannica*, 1824 (**511**), Lowndes's *Bibliographer's Manual*, 1857–64 (**371**), and Brunet's *Manuel du libraire et de l'amateur de livres*, 1860–80 (**513**) have their occasional usefulness today. Allibone, published 1858–91, has a wealth of out-of-the-way information on third- and tenth-rate writers that is collected nowhere else. So the rule should be: Scorn not the older book just because it is old. The newest book may indeed say all there is to be said on the subject—but not just because it is new.

Many reference books go through one or more revisions. Some revisions are so extensive that the preceding editions are entirely superseded. The first edition of Besterman, dated 1939–40, was lamentably incomplete, one reason being that it did not draw upon the extensive bibliographical collections of the Library of Congress. The second, dated 1947–49, was bigger and better, but suffered from the difficulties the bibliographer inevitably faced as a result of the war and its aftermath. The "third and final" edition, 1955–56, containing 80,000 entries as against the first edition's 42,000, was what the book should have been in the first place. Even so, the inexorable proliferation of bibliographical materials subsequently called forth still another—"this time really the last"—edition (1965–66), which listed 117,000 items. Again, the hand lists of plays that were an important feature of Nicoll's original series of volumes on the British drama from 1660 onward were very incomplete. These should now be consulted in their considerably expanded form, in the revised edition of the series (**173**).

"Revision" does not necessarily imply mere expansion, correction, and bringing up to date. It may also mean more or less sweeping changes of content. Certain articles that appear in one edition of that fascinating grab bag of historical odds and ends, *Haydn's Dictionary of Dates* (**882**), are missing from the next, and articles on different topics appear instead.

3. *Indexes.* To the traveler along the reference shelves, there is no more refreshing experience than to open a volume and behold a large, well-printed, and adequately subdivided index. But the

oasis may prove a brackish mirage if the indexing turns out to be defective. A quick and fairly accurate way of finding out whether an index may be used with confidence is to pick eight or ten names or subjects at random in the body of the book—not major references, but quite incidental ones, perhaps some occurring in lengthy lists— and then check on their accurate inclusion in the index. The conclusion to be drawn if none of them is there, or if some are there and others aren't, is obvious. Occasionally indexes are limited arbitrarily to certain kinds of material. In the indispensable Stationers' Register (784), for example, everybody connected with the printing and bookselling trades is indexed, but not the authors or titles of the thousands of books entered in the register.

If the work is in more than one volume, one must be sure to determine whether there is a reliable master index to the whole set, or whether each volume is indexed separately. A third possibility is that the indexing is done on some less common plan, such as one index for every two or three volumes. Here a knowledge of the publishing history of the set would prove valuable. It may never be assumed that a work lacks an index simply because the index is not in the usual place, at the end; in Bonamy Dobrée's six-volume edition of Lord Chesterfield's letters, published in 1932, the index to the whole set occurs in Volume I.

If a desired heading does not appear in an index, it always pays to look under various synonyms. Until fairly recently, most indexing was done on quite arbitrary and individualistic principles, so that if one failed to guess the exact word the indexer chose to designate a certain subject, he very possibly would not find the references he was looking for. Relatively few older books possess the elaborate and efficient system of cross-references to which the publications of the H. W. Wilson Company (*Readers' Guide, Humanities Index, Bibliographic Index,* etc.) have accustomed present-day researchers. The predecessor of these modern compilations, Poole's guide to nineteenth-century periodicals (680), scatters articles on a single broad subject under several headings, depending usually on the wording of the title. Thus, as the historian of the Wilson indexes reminds us, for a bibliography on the labor movement, Poole must be consulted under Labor, Associations of; Labor, Organized; Labor Associations; Labor Unions; Trade-Unionism; and Trade-Unions. On alcoholism one must look not only under that word but also under Alcoholic Excesses, the Drink Question, Drunkards, Drunkenness, Inebriates, Inebriety, Intemperance, Liquor, and Temperance.

In serial publications, comprehensive indexes of authors and titles are often provided at the end of a certain number of volumes. We have usually indicated the existence of such indexes in our entries for various periodicals. For a further useful guide, see Daniel C. Haskell, *A Check List of Cumulative Indexes to Individual Periodicals in the New York Public Library* (New York, 1942). One additional note: In the indexes to individual volumes and runs of some nineteenth-century periodicals, the alphabetization, once the initial letter of the word has been passed, is unpredictable, to say the least. LO may precede LE, and LA follow LI, with maddening insouciance.

4. *Plan.* Some works contain several alphabets or parts, each of which must be consulted in quest of a certain bit of information. There may be, for example, separate author, title, and subject alphabets. Or, as in the case of Peddie's *Subject Index* (**520**), each of four volumes may contain a complete alphabet as well as a brief supplementary one, making a total of eight to be consulted. Courtney's *Register* (**503**) has two alphabets: the first extending over Volumes I and II, the second in Volume III. Thus the hasty student, assuming that Peddie and Courtney have amassed all entries for the letter B in one place, is in danger of missing the very material for which he is searching. Again, to establish whether or not a certain rare piece of Americana is in the Library of Congress, one cannot stop with the main LC *Catalog of Books* (**313**); there are also several later alphabets to consult, in volumes of the *Catalog* published since 1946. (And, as a matter of fact, failure to find the item desired in any volume of the LC *Catalog* is not conclusive proof that the LC does not have it; for some very rare items, LC cards have never been printed. On the other hand, the LC *Catalog*, like its successor, the *National Union Catalog* (**314**), also contains entries for some books which are owned by other libraries but not by the Library of Congress itself.)

Some important bibliographical tools have other peculiarities of arrangement which must be understood before they can be satisfactorily used. In the Stationers' Register, a verbatim transcript of

various types of records of the Stationers' Company extending over
many decades, data relating to the publishing history of a certain
book, or the dealings of a bookseller, may have to be assembled
from several widely separated places. In Wells's *Manual of the
Writings in Middle English* (381) the main volume is divided into
two parts, one containing substantive information (dates, authorship, sources, contents, etc. of literary works) and the other containing bibliographical references. This division is maintained
throughout the nine supplements, and the reference system by
which the supplements are tied to each other and to the parent
volume calls for patient mastery before use.

  5. *Accuracy.* A reference work that is inconveniently arranged
is a nuisance, but with persistence it may be forced to yield up its
quota of information. A work that is unreliable, however, presents
problems that are both more subtle and more sinister. If the data
the scholar collects are inaccurate, the whole process of research is
endangered.

  The sources and occasions of error in reference books, needless
to say, are manifold. From the modern scholarly point of view,
among the most culpable of sins is the uncritical adoption of somebody else's "facts." This, apart from justifiable indignation over
the chaotic arrangement, is the main charge against W. Carew
Hazlitt's series of bibliographies of pre-1700 English literature
(382). Especially in the earliest volumes, Hazlitt depended too
freely on the kindness of friends at Oxford and Cambridge, who
favored him with much imprecise information that he never both-
ered to verify. (It is also said that much of Hazlitt's undepend-
ability can be traced to his habit of making notes on the backs of
old envelopes, but since this is a standard libel among scholars, it
may be no more true of Hazlitt than of some other bibliographers.)
Block's bibliography of the English novel (422) likewise has been
severely criticized for its reliance on secondary sources such as the
British Museum Catalogue and booksellers' catalogues, without any
systematic attempt to examine the books themselves. Nowadays
the best practice requires that, except in the most extraordinary circumstances, the bibliographer *see* every book he lists; otherwise
there is always the chance that his pages will harbor a few bibliographical ghosts. Blanck's great *Bibliography of American Liter-*

ature (**442**) is being constructed on that admirable principle. A corollary rule requires that the student transcribe the author, title, and publishing information of any book he cites from the title page itself, rather than from any bibliographical reference. Some reference books are seriously unreliable in their presentation of titles. In Poole's *Index,* for example, the titles of some periodical articles are not identical with those found in the magazines themselves, and in Malclès' *Les Sources du travail bibliographique* (**494**) some of the standard works included in the present handbook are incorrectly listed.

How can the student guard against being misled by his reference sources? One way is to find out the editor's or compiler's general reputation for dependability. Unfortunately there is no bibliographical Dun and Bradstreet that lists scholarly credit ratings. All one can do is to be constantly alert for remarks made in other books or dropped by one's teachers in lectures or seminar discussions. By keeping his eyes and ears open, the student of Elizabethan drama, for instance, will soon become aware that F. G. Fleay (1831–1909) is notorious for his wild surmises, and that to cite him as a sole authority for any statement is an act of naiveté. In such works as Sheehy's *Guide to Reference Books* (**495**), critical evaluations are made of many of the books listed here. But the standards by which professional librarians judge the dependability of reference books are, necessarily, more lenient than those employed by specialists in any field of learning; so that many a book which is perfectly serviceable for the ordinary library patron is not reliable enough for the stern requirements of the expert.

Another way to learn the standing of a research tool, particularly a specialized one in the field of literary scholarship, is to look up the scholarly reviews. Everyone who has frequent occasion to use the *NCBEL* (**372**) would do well to consult a few of the extensive reviews that followed its publication. See, for example, the severe critique of Volume III in *JEGP,* 70 (1971), 139–45.

6. *Thoroughness and bias.* Relatively few research tools approach absolute exhaustiveness on their chosen subject. Thus it is always desirable to know, either from the editor's explicit statements or by inference from the contents, the circumstances that have limited a work's scope or affected its emphasis. Many bibliogra-

phies of individual authors or of specific types have been based, not
upon a wide-ranging canvass of many libraries, but upon a single
collection.   Perhaps the most famous recent example of this is the
sumptuous catalogue of "nineteenth-century" (actually in great part
Victorian) fiction by Michael Sadleir (**423**), which, as the subtitle
says, is based on his own collection.   Valuable though the two volumes are, they cannot be regarded as exhaustive or comprehensive,
since their contents were determined by Sadleir's personal tastes as
a collector and his luck in acquiring copies of books notoriously
difficult to collect.

Any work to which many hands contribute is bound to be uneven.
The disproportion between many sections of the *NCBEL* is well
known.   Some sections, such as those on the history of printing and
publishing and on periodicals, are among the best available bibliographical guides to their subjects.   Others are so highly selective,
or even capricious, as to be virtually worthless for the purposes of
serious research.   As is true of Spiller's *Literary History* and numerous other collaborative enterprises, the value of any particular
section depends on the conscientiousness and expertness of the man
or woman who produced it.

National origin accounts for considerable imbalance in certain
reference works.   *The Year's Work in English Studies* (**454**), which
has a staff of British contributors, often neglects American scholarly
productions of distinctly greater importance than some British
works that receive more extended treatment.   Mlle. Malclès places
greatest stress on the bibliographical and reference tools of European countries, particularly France, while Mr. Sheehy emphasizes
American ones—in both cases an understandable, and in practical
terms entirely defensible, bias.   Less defensible, perhaps, is the
heavy predominance of the work of German scholars and critics in
books like Hans Eppelsheimer's *Handbuch der Weltliteratur*.   In
any event, which there is a choice of sources to be consulted, one
must take into account the likelihood that the fullest and most
authoritative treatment of materials pertaining to a certain country
will be found in a reference work originating there.   This is less
true, of course, in the field of literary studies, where so many of the
"standard" books on English literature have been produced by
Americans.

Again, there is the question of the audience or market for which the work was intended. The variety of author bibliographies illustrates the point. Some bibliographies of this kind were compiled primarily to help librarians strengthen their collections of the authors' works. They are therefore little more than "check lists," and have relatively minor research usefulness. Others were designed especially for collectors, many of whom are sentimentalists rather than scholars. Sometimes they contain much valuable material, but to find the grain requires much sifting out of chaff. (An example is William Miller's voluminous *The Dickens Student and Collector* [Cambridge, Mass., 1946], which is uncritical in the extreme and disfigured by many errors.*) In a similar category are author bibliographies compiled by booksellers. These are often more accurately described as catalogues of individual collections which the dealer has either amassed himself or purchased *en bloc*. Obviously they are not exhaustive; and their emphasis consistently is on the features of the books or manuscripts which enhance their market value—features that are not always those who interest the scholar. Finally, there are author bibliographies intended specifically for scholarly use, compiled by persons who, at least theoretically, know what scholars need and want. Abstractly considered, these should always be the most valuable kind of reference tool. But in practice such is not always the case, simply because, as everywhere else in life, the quality of performance varies from person to person.

And so we return to the point from which we started: No single book recorded in the following pages is perfect, because no man or combination of men is infallible. The ultimate worth of any reference work depends on its maker's devotion, intelligence, erudition, and access to materials, and above all on the degree to which he has been able to harness these advantages to produce a work that is at once authoritative and convenient to use. It is not a simple task for the student to estimate how successful the compiler has been. But the more shrewdly he evaluates every book he uses, the more efficient and fruitful his own program of research will turn out to be.

* See Philo Calhoun and Howell J. Heaney, "Dickensiana in the Rough," *PBSA*, 41 (1947), 293–320.

SOME ABBREVIATIONS COMMONLY USED BY LITERARY SCHOLARS

For an exhaustive list of abbreviations of periodicals, see the MLA International Bibliography (**453**).

AL	*American Literature*
BAL	(Blanck's) *Bibliography of American Literature*
BL	The British Library
BM	The British Museum
CBEL	*The Cambridge Bibliography of English Literature*
CBI	*Cumulative Book Index*
DAB	*Dictionary of American Biography*
DAE	*A Dictionary of American English*
DNB	*Dictionary of National Biography*
ELH	*ELH: A Journal of English Literary History* *
ELN	*English Language Notes*
JEGP	*JEGP: Journal of English and Germanic Philology*
JHI	*Journal of the History of Ideas*
LC	The Library of Congress
LHUS	*Literary History of the United States*
MHRA	The Modern Humanities Research Association
MLA	The Modern Language Association of America
MLN	*Modern Language Notes*
MLQ	*Modern Language Quarterly*
MLR	*Modern Language Review*
MP	*Modern Philology*
N&Q	*Notes and Queries*
NCBEL	*The New Cambridge Bibliography of English Literature*
NUC	*The National Union Catalog*
OED	*The Oxford English Dictionary*
PBSA	*Papers of the Bibliographical Society of America*
PMLA	*PMLA: Publications of the Modern Language Association of America*
PQ	*Philological Quarterly*
PRO	The Public Record Office (London)
RES	*The Review of English Studies*
SB	*Studies in Bibliography*
SP	*Studies in Philology*
STC	*Short-Title Catalogue*
TLS	*TLS: The [London] Times Literary Supplement*
ULS	*Union List of Serials*
YWES	*The Year's Work in English Studies*

* In 1956 the subtitle was dropped.

11

THE SCOPE, AIMS, AND METHODS OF
LITERARY SCHOLARSHIP

1 WELLEK, RENÉ, and AUSTIN WARREN. Theory of Literature. 3rd ed. New York, [1963].

2 ALTICK, RICHARD D. The Scholar Adventurers. New York, 1950. Read 4/78

3 SHERBURN, GEORGE. "Words That Intimidate." *PMLA*, 65 (1950), No. 1, pp. 3–12.

4 JONES, HOWARD MUMFORD. One Great Society: Humane Learning in the United States. New York, 1959.
See especially Chapters 6, 7, and 11.

5 WHALLEY, GEORGE. "Scholarship and Criticism." University of Toronto Quarterly, 29 (1959/60), 33–45.

6 BUSH, DOUGLAS. "Literary Scholarship and Criticism." Liberal Education, 47 (1961), 207–28.

7 The Aims and Methods of Scholarship in Modern Languages and Literatures, ed. James Thorpe. 2nd ed. New York, 1970.

8 DAICHES, DAVID. English Literature. Englewood Cliffs, N.J., 1964.

9 The Morality of Scholarship, ed. Max Black. Ithaca, 1967.
Essays by Northrop Frye, Stuart Hampshire, and Conor Cruise O'Brien.

10 Relations of Literary Study: Essays on Interdisciplinary Contributions, ed. James Thorpe. New York, 1967.

11 WATSON, GEORGE. The Study of Literature. London, 1969.

BIBLIOGRAPHICAL HANDBOOKS

13 BOND, DONALD F. A Reference Guide to English Studies. 2nd ed. Chicago, 1971.

14 KENNEDY, ARTHUR G., and DONALD B. SANDS. A Concise Bibliography for Students of English. 5th ed., revised by William E. Colburn. Stanford, 1972.

15 BATESON, F. W., and HARRISON T. MESEROLE. A Guide to English and American Literature. 3rd ed. New York, 1976.

16 WRIGHT, ANDREW. A Reader's Guide to English and American Literature. Chicago, 1970.

17 KEHLER, DOROTHEA, and FIDELIA DICKINSON. Problems in Literary Research. Metuchen, N.J., 1975.

18 PATTERSON, MARGARET. Literary Research Guide. Detroit, 1976.

19 SCHWEIK, ROBERT C., and DIETER RIESNER. Reference Sources in English and American Literature. New York, 1977.

THE TECHNIQUES OF RESEARCH

23 BARZUN, JACQUES, and HENRY F. GRAFF. The Modern Researcher. 3rd ed. New York, 1977.

24 ALTICK, RICHARD D. The Art of Literary Research. 2nd ed. New York, 1975. Read 9/78

24a BATESON, F. W. The Scholar-Critic. London, 1972.

25 BEAURLINE, LESTER A., ed. A Mirror for Modern Scholars: Essays in Methods of Research in Literature. New York, 1966.

26 ZITNER, SHELDON P., ed. The Practice of Modern Literary Scholarship. Chicago, 1966.

27 WINKS, ROBIN W., ed. The Historian as Detective: Essays on Evidence. New York, 1969.

SCHOLARLY STYLE

29 McKERROW, R. B. "Form and Matter in the Publication of Research." *RES*, 16 (1940), 116–21.
   Reprinted in *PMLA*, 65 (1950), No. 3, pp. 3–8.

30 SILVER, HENRY M. "Putting It on Paper." *PMLA*, 65 (1950), No. 3, pp. 9–20.

31 NICHOLSON, MARGARET.   A Practical Style Guide for Authors and Editors.   New York, 1967.

32 COLLISON, R. L.   Indexes and Indexing.   4th ed.   London, 1972.

33 UNIVERSITY OF CHICAGO PRESS.   A Manual of Style.   12th ed.   Chicago, 1969.

34 MLA Handbook for Writers of Research Papers, Theses, and Dissertations.   New York, 1977.
    Replaces the MLA Style Sheet.

(23) BARZUN, JACQUES, and HENRY F. GRAFF.   The Modern Researcher.   3rd ed.   New York, 1977.
    See Part 3.

LITERARY ENCYCLOPEDIAS AND HANDBOOKS
English and American

39 ALLIBONE, S. AUSTIN.   A Critical Dictionary of English Literature and British and American Authors.   3 vols.   Philadelphia, 1858–71.   Supplement.   2 vols.   Philadelphia, 1891.
    The usefulness of this work is too often underestimated.

40 [GHOSH, J. C.]   Annals of English Literature 1475–1950.   2nd ed. [revised by R. W. Chapman et al.]   Oxford, 1961.
    For more detailed chronologies, see the various volumes of the Oxford History of English Literature (71); the Oxford Companion to American Literature (43); VAN TIEGHEM (61); and, for the broader historical context, MAYER (884), GRUN (884a), STOREY (884b), and WILLIAMS (885, 886).

40a Crowell's Handbook of Elizabethan and Stuart Literature, ed. James E. Ruoff.   New York, 1975.

41 The Oxford Companion to English Literature, ed. Paul Harvey.   4th ed., revised by Dorothy Eagle.   Oxford, 1967.

42 The New Century Handbook of English Literature, ed. Clarence L. Barnhart.   Revised ed.   New York, 1967.

42a Longman Companion to English Literature, ed. Christopher Gillie.   London, 1972.

43 The Oxford Companion to American Literature, ed. James D. Hart. 4th ed. New York, 1965.

PS 21 .H3

44 BURKE, W. J., and WILL D. HOWE. American Authors and Books 1640 to the Present Day. 3rd ed., revised by Irving Weiss and Anne Weiss. New York, 1972.

Z 1224 .B87

> The original edition (New York, 1943) contains much material not included in the current edition.

45 HERZBERG, MAX J., et al. The Reader's Encyclopedia of American Literature. New York, 1962.

(REF) PS 21 .R4

General, Classical, and Modern European

46 SHIPLEY, JOSEPH T. Encyclopedia of Literature. 2 vols. New York, 1946.

47 ———. Dictionary of World Literary Terms. 3rd ed. Boston, 1970.

> Former title: Dictionary of World Literature.

48 Cassell's Encyclopaedia of World Literature, ed. S. H. Steinberg. Revised edition. 3 vols. New York, 1973.

49 The Penguin Companion to Literature, ed. David Daiches et al. 4 vols. London, 1969–71.

50 BENÉT, WILLIAM ROSE. The Reader's Encyclopedia. 2nd ed. New York, 1965.

51 Princeton Encyclopedia of Poetry and Poetics, ed. Alex Preminger et al. Enlarged ed. Princeton, 1974.

(REF) PN 1021 .E5 c2

> Formerly titled Encyclopedia of Poetry and Poetics.

(includes lists of terms)

52 THOMPSON, STITH. Motif-Index of Folk-Literature. Revised ed. 6 vols. Bloomington, 1955–58.

53 Funk & Wagnalls Standard Dictionary of Folklore, Mythology and Legend, ed. Maria Leach and Jerome Fried. 2 vols. New York, 1949–50.

53a Brewer's Dictionary of Phrase and Fable, revised by Ivor H. Evans. London, 1970.

54 ATKINS, J. W. H. Literary Criticism in Antiquity. 2 vols. Cambridge, 1934.

55 THOMSON, J. A. K. The Classical Background of English Literature. London, 1948.

56 HIGHET, GILBERT. The Classical Tradition: Greek and Roman Influences on Western Literature. Oxford, 1949.

57 Concise Encyclopedia of Greek and Roman Mythology, ed. Sabine G. Oswalt. Chicago, 1969.

58 HADAS, MOSES. Ancilla to Classical Reading. New York, 1954.

59 The New Century Classical Handbook, ed. Catherine B. Avery. New York, 1962.

60 The Oxford Classical Dictionary, ed. N. G. L. Hammond and H. H. Scullard. 2nd ed. Oxford, 1970.

61 Répertoire chronologique des littératures modernes, ed. Paul Van Tieghem. Paris, 1935–37.
    See also ANTONY BRETT-JAMES, The Triple Stream: Four Centuries of English, French, and German Literature, 1531–1930 (Cambridge, 1953).

62 Columbia Dictionary of Modern European Literature, ed. Horatio Smith. New York, 1947.

62a Longman Companion to Twentieth Century Literature, ed. A. C. Ward. 2nd ed. London, 1975.

63 The Oxford Companion to French Literature, ed. Paul Harvey and J. E. Heseltine. Oxford, 1959.

63a The Oxford Companion to German Literature, ed. Henry and Mary Garland. Oxford, 1976.

64 The Oxford Companion to the Theatre, ed. Phyllis Hartnoll. 3rd ed. London, 1967.

65 Crowell's Handbook of Contemporary Drama, ed. Michael Anderson et al. New York, 1971.

66 McGraw-Hill Encyclopedia of World Drama. 4 vols. New York, 1972.

67 Modern World Drama: An Encyclopedia, ed. Myron Matlaw. New York, 1972.

ENGLISH LITERATURE: General Histories

71 The Oxford History of English Literature. Oxford, 1945– .
Of the fourteen projected volumes, these have so far been issued:
II. Part 1. H. S. BENNETT. Chaucer and the Fifteenth Century. 1947.
II. Part 2. E. K. CHAMBERS. English Literature at the Close of the Middle Ages. 1945.
III. C. S. LEWIS. English Literature in the Sixteenth Century. Excluding Drama. 1954.
IV. Part 1. F. P. WILSON. The English Drama 1485–1585. 1969.
✓ V. DOUGLAS BUSH. English Literature in the Earlier Seventeenth Century 1600–1660. 2nd ed. 1962.
VI. JAMES SUTHERLAND. English Literature in the Late Seventeenth Century. 1969.
VII. BONAMY DOBRÉE. English Literature in the Earlier Eighteenth Century. 1959.
IX. W. L. RENWICK. English Literature 1789–1815. 1963.
X. IAN JACK. English Literature 1815–1832. 1963.
XII. J. I. M. STEWART. Eight Modern Writers. 1963.

72 BAUGH, ALBERT C., et al. A Literary History of England. New York, 1948.
The second edition (1967) contains extensive bibliographical supplements.

ENGLISH LITERATURE: Period Histories

Anglo-Saxon Period

82 KENNEDY, CHARLES W. The Earliest English Poetry. New York, 1943.

83 GREENFIELD, STANLEY B. A Critical History of Old English Literature. New York, 1965.

Middle English Period

89 KER, W. P. English Literature Mediaeval. London, 1912.
Recent reprints are titled Medieval English Literature.

90 SCHLAUCH, MARGARET. English Medieval Literature and Its Social Foundations. Warsaw, 1956.

91 LEWIS, C. S. The Allegory of Love: A Study in Medieval Tradition. Revised ed. London, 1938.

92 KANE, GEORGE. Middle English Literature: A Critical Study of the Romances, the Religious Lyrics, Piers Plowman. London, 1951.

93 LOOMIS, ROGER SHERMAN, ed. Arthurian Literature in the Middle Ages: A Collaborative History. Oxford, 1959.

The Renaissance

99 GRIERSON, HERBERT J. C. Cross Currents in English Literature of the Seventeenth Century. London, 1929.

100 WEDGWOOD, C. V. Seventeenth-Century English Literature. 2nd ed. London, 1970.

The Restoration and Eighteenth Century

107 STEPHEN, LESLIE. English Literature and Society in the Eighteenth Century. London, 1904.

108 ELTON, OLIVER. A Survey of English Literature, 1730–1780. 2 vols. London, 1928.

109 SHERBURN, GEORGE. The Restoration and Eighteenth Century (1660–1789). (Baugh, A Literary History of England [72], Book III.)

110 GREENE, DONALD. The Age of Exuberance. New York, 1970.

The Nineteenth Century

116 ELTON, OLIVER. A Survey of English Literature, 1780–1830. 2 vols. London, 1912.

117 ———. A Survey of English Literature, 1830–1880. 2 vols. London, 1920.

118 BUCKLEY, JEROME HAMILTON. The Victorian Temper. Cambridge, Mass., 1951.

The Twentieth Century

123 TINDALL, WILLIAM YORK. Forces in Modern British Literature, 1885–1956. New York, 1956.

124 DAICHES, DAVID. The Present Age After 1920. (Introductions to English Literature, Vol. V.) London, 1958.

125 FRASER, G. S. The Modern Writer and His World. Revised ed. New York, 1965.

ENGLISH LITERATURE: Special Topics

Linguistics

131 BAUGH, ALBERT C. A History of the English Language. 2nd ed. New York, 1957.

132 BLOOMFIELD, LEONARD. Language. New York, 1933.

133 HOCKETT, CHARLES F. A Course in Modern Linguistics. New York, 1958.

134 ROBINS, R. H. A Short History of Linguistics. London, 1968.

Folklore

137 KRAPPE, ALEXANDER HAGGERTY. The Science of Folk-Lore. London, 1930.

138 GEROULD, GORDON H. The Ballad of Tradition. New York, 1932.

139 THOMPSON, STITH. The Folktale. New York, 1946.

Stylistics

141 HOUGH, GRAHAM. Style and Stylistics. London, 1969.

History of Criticism

145 SAINTSBURY, GEORGE. A History of English Criticism. Edinburgh, 1911.
  The English sections of the author's three-volume History of Criticism and Literary Taste in Europe (Edinburgh, 1900–04).

146 ATKINS, J. W. H. English Literary Criticism: The Medieval Phase. New York, 1943.

147 ———. English Literary Criticism: The Renascence. 2nd ed. London, 1951.

148 ATKINS, J. W. H.   English Literary Criticism: Seventeenth and Eighteenth Centuries.   London, 1951.

> For important strictures on Atkins as well as an excellent introduction to the difficulties of writing histories of criticism, see R. S. CRANE, "On Writing the History of English Criticism, 1650–1800," University of Toronto Quarterly, 22 (1952/3), 376–91.

149 ABRAMS, M. H.   The Mirror and the Lamp: Romantic Theory and the Critical Tradition.   New York, 1953.

150 WELLEK, RENÉ.   A History of Modern Criticism: 1750–1950. New Haven, 1955– .

> To be completed in five volumes, of which the first four have been published.

151 WIMSATT, WILLIAM K., JR., and CLEANTH BROOKS.   Literary Criticism: A Short History.   New York, 1957.

> Controversial.   See *PQ*, 37 (1958), 307–09, and 38 (1959), 299, for listing of representative reviews.

152 WATSON, GEORGE.   The Literary Critics.   London, 1962.

History of Poetry

157 COURTHOPE, W. J.   A History of English Poetry.   6 vols. London, 1895–1910.

158 BUSH, DOUGLAS.   Mythology and the Renaissance Tradition in English Poetry.   Revised ed.   New York, 1963.

159 ———.   Mythology and the Romantic Tradition in English Poetry.   Cambridge, Mass., 1937.

160 PERKINS, DAVID.   A History of Modern Poetry from the 1890's to the High Modernist Mode.   Cambridge, Mass., 1976– .

> To be completed in two volumes.   The first volume carries the history to the mid-1920's; the second volume will go to the present.

History of Drama

166 HARBAGE, ALFRED.   Annals of English Drama 975–1700. Revised ed. by Samuel Schoenbaum.   Philadelphia, 1964. Supplement.   Evanston, Ill., 1966.   Second supplement. Evanston, Ill., 1970.

John Genest — 10 vols on London Stage
(pub in 19th century)

Odell — Annals of
^ NY Stage   (American)

167 NICOLL, ALLARDYCE. British Drama: An Historical Survey from the Beginnings to the Present Time. 5th ed. New York, 1962.

167a The Revels History of Drama in English, ed. Clifford Leech et al. New York, 1975– .
   To be published in eight volumes, of which four have been issued to date.

168 CHAMBERS, E. K. The Mediaeval Stage. 2 vols. Oxford, 1903.

169 YOUNG, KARL. The Drama of the Medieval Church. 2 vols. Oxford, 1933.

170 CRAIG, HARDIN. English Religious Drama of the Middle Ages. Oxford, 1955.

171 CHAMBERS, E. K. The Elizabethan Stage. 4 vols. Oxford, 1923.
   Index by BEATRICE WHITE (Oxford, 1934).

172 BENTLEY, GERALD EADES. The Jacobean and Caroline Stage. 7 vols. Oxford, 1941–68.

173 NICOLL, ALLARDYCE. A History of English Drama, 1660–1900. Revised ed. 6 vols. Cambridge, 1952–59.
   Originally published under separate titles in seven volumes, 1923–46. Continued by the same author's English Drama 1900–1930: The Beginnings of the Modern Period (Cambridge, 1973).

174 VAN LENNEP, WILLIAM. The London Stage 1660–1800: A *PN 2592 .L6* Calendar of Plays, Entertainments & Afterpieces Together with Casts, Box-Receipts and Contemporary Comment. 5 parts in 11 vols. Carbondale, Ill., 1960–68. *w/ Index*

   ¶ *See also* PHILIP HIGHFILL, JR., et al., A Biographical Dictionary of Actors, Actresses, Musicians, Dancers, Managers, *incomplete at UWM — not all pub.* and Other Stage Personnel in London, 1660–1800 (Carbondale, Ill., 1973–).

History of Fiction

179 BAKER, ERNEST A. The History of the English Novel. 10 vols. London, 1924–39. Vol. XI, by Lionel Stevenson. New York, 1967.

180 ALLEN, WALTER. The English Novel: A Short Critical History. London, 1954.

181 WATT, IAN. The Rise of the Novel: Studies in Defoe, Richardson, and Fielding. London, 1957.

182 STEVENSON, LIONEL. The English Novel: A Panorama. Boston, 1960.

183 ALLEN, WALTER. The Modern Novel in Britain and the United States. New York, 1963.

AMERICAN LITERATURE: General Histories

188 SPILLER, ROBERT E., et al., eds. Literary History of the United States. 4th ed. 2 vols. New York, 1974. (*"LHUS"*)

189 LÜDEKE, HENRY. Geschichte der amerikanischen Literatur. Bern, 1952.

190 CUNLIFFE, MARCUS. The Literature of the United States. 3rd ed. London, 1967.

AMERICAN LITERATURE: Period Histories

The Colonies and the Early Republic

197 TYLER, MOSES COIT. A History of American Literature, 1607–1765. 2 vols. New York, 1878.

198 ———. The Literary History of the American Revolution, 1763–1783. 2 vols. New York, 1897.

199 MILLER, PERRY. The New England Mind: From Colony to Province. Cambridge, Mass., 1953.

200 ———. The New England Mind: The Seventeenth Century. New York, 1939.

The Nineteenth Century

206 MATTHIESSEN, F. O. American Renaissance. New York, 1941.

The Twentieth Century

212 KAZIN, ALFRED. On Native Grounds: An Interpretation of Modern American Prose Literature. New York, 1942.

213 STRAUMANN, HEINRICH. American Literature in the Twentieth Century. 3rd ed. New York, 1965.

AMERICAN LITERATURE: Special Topics
Linguistics

219 KRAPP, GEORGE PHILIP. The English Language in America. 2 vols. New York, 1925.

220 MENCKEN, H. L. The American Language. 4th ed. New York, 1936. Supplements One and Two. New York, 1945–48.

221 FRANCIS, W. NELSON. The Structure of American English. New York, 1958.

Folklore

(139) THOMPSON, STITH. The Folktale. New York, 1946.

History of Criticism

233 FOERSTER, NORMAN. American Criticism. Boston, 1928.

234 JONES, HOWARD MUMFORD. The Theory of American Literature. 2nd ed. Ithaca, 1965.

235 O'CONNOR, WILLIAM VAN. An Age of Criticism 1900–1950. Chicago, 1952.

History of Poetry

241 PEARCE, ROY HARVEY. The Continuity of American Poetry. Princeton, 1961.

(160) PERKINS, DAVID. A History of Modern Poetry from the 1890's to the High Modernist Mode. Cambridge, Mass., 1976– .
    To be completed in two volumes. The first volume carries the history to the mid-1920's; the second volume will go to the present.

242 WAGGONER, HYATT H. American Poets from the Puritans to the Present Day. Boston, 1968.

243 GELPI, ALBERT. The Tenth Muse: The Psyche of the American Poet. Cambridge, Mass., 1975.

History of Drama

247 QUINN, ARTHUR HOBSON. A History of the American Drama from the Beginning to the Civil War. New York, 1923.

248 ———. A History of the American Drama from the Civil War to the Present Day. 2 vols. New York, 1927.
Revised edition in one volume, 1936.

249 BOGARD, TRAVIS, et al. American Drama. New York, 1977.
Issued as Vol. 8 of The Revels History of the Drama in English (**167a**).

History of Fiction

254 QUINN, ARTHUR HOBSON. American Fiction: An Historical and Critical Survey. New York, 1936.

255 COWIE, ALEXANDER. The Rise of the American Novel. New York, 1948.

✓ 256 CHASE, RICHARD. The American Novel and Its Tradition. New York, 1957.

(183) ALLEN, WALTER. The Modern Novel in Britain and the United States. New York, 1963.

CULTURAL AND INTELLECTUAL HISTORY

European and English

263 RANDALL, JOHN HERMAN, JR. The Making of the Modern Mind. Revised ed. New York, 1940.

264 BRINTON, CRANE. Ideas and Men: The Story of Western Thought. New York, 1950.

265 BOLGAR, R. R. The Classical Heritage and Its Beneficiaries. Cambridge, 1954.

266 CASPARI, FRITZ. Humanism and the Social Order in Tudor England. Chicago, 1954.

267 WILLEY, BASIL. The Seventeenth Century Background. London, 1934.

268 LOVEJOY, ARTHUR O. The Great Chain of Being. Cambridge, Mass., 1936.

269 BECKER, CARL L. The Heavenly City of the Eighteenth Century Philosophers. New Haven, 1932.

270 GAY, PETER. The Enlightenment: An Interpretation. 2 vols. New York, 1966–69.

271 WILLEY, BASIL. The Eighteenth Century Background. London, 1940.

272 HOUGHTON, WALTER E. The Victorian Frame of Mind, 1830–1870. New Haven, 1957.

273 ALTICK, RICHARD D. Victorian People and Ideas: A Companion for the Modern Reader of Victorian Literature. New York, 1973.

274 WHITEHEAD, ALFRED NORTH. Science and the Modern World. New York, 1925.

American

278 PARRINGTON, VERNON LOUIS. Main Currents in American Thought. 3 vols. New York, 1927–30.

(206) MATTHIESSEN, F. O. American Renaissance. New York, 1941.

279 COMMAGER, HENRY STEELE. The American Mind. New Haven, 1950.

280 CURTI, MERLE. The Growth of American Thought. 3rd ed. New York, 1964.

GUIDES TO LIBRARIES: American
General

287 DOWNS, ROBERT B. American Library Resources: A Bibliographical Guide. Chicago, 1951. Supplements. 2 vols. Chicago, 1962, 1972.

288 ASH, LEE, WILLIAM MILLER, and ALFRED WALTERMIRE, JR. Subject Collections: A Guide to Special Book Collections and Subject Emphases as Reported by University, College, Public, and Special Libraries and Museums in the United States and Canada. 4th ed. New York, 1974.

¶ See also **858–861**.

Individual

298 **Harvard.** See file of the Harvard Library Bulletin (653) and The Houghton Library 1942–1967: A Selection of Books and Manuscripts in Harvard Collections (Cambridge, Mass., 1967).

299 **Yale.** See file of the Yale University Library Gazette, 1926– . (Cumulative index, Vols. 1–31.) See also WIL-MARTH S. LEWIS, The Yale Collections (New Haven, 1946), pp. 1–13.
> Volume 48, No. 4 (1974) is devoted to "The Beinecke Rare Book and Manuscript Room: A Guide to Its Collections."

300 **American Antiquarian Society.** See CLARENCE S. BRIGHAM, Fifty Years of Collecting Americana (Worcester, Mass., 1958).

301 **John Carter Brown Library.** See LAWRENCE C. WROTH, The First Century of the John Carter Brown Library (Providence, R.I., 1946).

302 **New York Public Library.** See SAM P. WILLIAMS, Guide to the Research Collections of the New York Public Library (Chicago, 1975); and Dictionary Catalog of the Henry W. and Albert A. Berg Collection of English and American Literature (5 vols., Boston, 1969).

303 **The Morgan Library.** See FREDERICK B. ADAMS, An Introduction to the Pierpont Morgan Library (revised ed., New York, 1974).

304 **Library of Congress.** See CHARLES A. GOODRUM, The Library of Congress (Washington, 1974).

305 **The Folger Library.** See JOSEPH QUINCY ADAMS, The Folger Shakespeare Memorial Library (Washington, 1942); JAMES G. McMANAWAY, "The Folger Shakespeare Library," Shakespeare Survey 1 (1948), 57–78; LOUIS B. WRIGHT, The Folger Library: Two Decades of Growth (Charlottesville, 1968); and Catalog of Printed Books of the Folger Shakespeare Library (28 vols., Boston, 1970).
> For the Folger's manuscripts, see **862a**.

306 **Newberry Library.** See LAWRENCE W. TOWNER, An Uncommon Collection of Uncommon Collections: The Newberry Library (2nd ed., Chicago, 1976).

307 **University of Texas Library.** See file of the Library Chronicle of the University of Texas, 1944– , and A Creative Century: Selections from the Twentieth Century Collections at the University of Texas (Austin, 1964).

308 **Huntington Library.** See surveys of holdings in Huntington Library Bulletin, No. 1 (1931), 33–104, and Huntington Library Quarterly, 3 (1939), 131–45; GODFREY DAVIES, "The Huntington Library," Shakespeare Survey 6 (1953), 53–63; and SCHULZ (**862**).

Catalogues

313 A Catalog of Books Represented by Library of Congress Printed Cards Issued to July 31, 1942.   167 vols.   Ann Arbor, 1942–46.   ("LC Catalog")
Supplement: Cards Issued August 1, 1942–December 31, 1947.   42 vols.   Ann Arbor, 1948.

   Continued as follows:

The Library of Congress Author Catalog [1948–52].   24 vols.   Ann Arbor, 1953.

The National Union Catalog: 1952–1955 Imprints: An Author List.   30 vols.   Ann Arbor, 1961.

The National Union Catalog: A Cumulative Author List, 1953–57.   28 vols.   Ann Arbor, 1958.
   Unlike the preceding set, a union catalog only for 1956–57; otherwise limited to LC acquisitions.

The National Union Catalog: A Cumulative Author List. Washington, 1956– .
   The open-end continuation of **314**. Published monthly; cumulated quarterly, annually, and at five-year intervals (1958–62, 1963–67, etc.).

314 The National Union Catalog: Pre-1956 Imprints.   About 610 vols. London, 1968– .   (*"NUC"*)
   When completed, will supersede all except the last of the preceding series.

315 Library of Congress and National Union Catalog Author Lists, 1942–1962: A Master Cumulation. 152 vols. Detroit, 1969–70.
> An interim cumulation, being superseded by **314** and its serial continuation.

¶ Many American libraries issued printed catalogues in the nineteenth century; these are often useful for bibliographical information as well as for locating copies. In addition, there are many valuable catalogues of special collections in public, college, and university libraries. For these, see DOWNS (**287**).

GUIDES TO LIBRARIES: British

General

327 DOWNS, ROBERT B. British Library Resources: A Bibliographical Guide. Chicago, 1973.

328 ASLIB Directory, ed. Brian J. Wilson. 3rd ed. 2 vols. London, 1968–70.
> Volume II lists collections in the humanities and the social sciences.

329 RYE, REGINALD ARTHUR. The Students' Guide to the Libraries of London. 3rd ed. London, 1927.

330 IRWIN, RAYMOND, and RONALD STAVELY, eds. The Libraries of London. 2nd ed. London, 1961.
> Supplements but does not replace **329**.

The British Library *

337 ESDAILE, ARUNDELL. The British Museum Library: A Short History and Survey. London, 1946.
> See also *TLS*, June 17 and 24, 1955, pp. 338, 356.

338 BRITISH MUSEUM. General Catalogue of Printed Books. Photolithographic Edition to 1955. 263 vols. London, 1959–66. Decennial Supplement 1956–65. 50 vols. London, 1968.

(*Entry continued on next page.*)

* Formerly, the British Museum.

On the peculiarities of the cataloguing system, see Rules for Compiling the Catalogues in the Department of Printed Books in the British Museum (2nd ed., London, 1936). In the present catalogue, however, titles entered under "Academies" in former editions have been distributed according to geographical location, and the 26-letter alphabet has been adopted (entries beginning with I and J were formerly merged under one letter, as were those beginning with U and V).

339 FRANCIS, F. C. "The Catalogues of the British Museum. 1. Printed Books." Journal of Documentation, 4 (1948), 14–40.

340 SKEAT, T. C. "The Catalogues of the British Museum. 2. Manuscripts." Journal of Documentation, 7 (1951), 18–60. Revised edition, published separately (London, 1962).

Z
6621
.B844

The London Library

345 Catalogue of the London Library. 2 vols. London, 1913–14. Supplements, 1913–50. 3 vols. London, 1920–53.
See also SIMON NOWELL-SMITH, "London Library Occasions," *TLS*, February 18, 1972, pp. 187–88.

The John Rylands Library

351 [DUFF, E. GORDON.] Catalogue of the Printed Books and Manuscripts in the John Rylands Library. 3 vols. Manchester, 1899.
See also the Bulletin of the John Rylands Library (1903–   ).

University Libraries

357 NEWCOMBE, LUXMOORE. The University and College Libraries of Great Britain and Ireland. London, 1927.

358 MUNBY, A. N. L. Cambridge College Libraries: Aids for Research Students. 2nd ed. Cambridge, 1962.

359 MORGAN, PAUL. Oxford Libraries Outside the Bodleian. Oxford, 1973.

A series of authoritative articles on great British libraries appeared in *TLS*, as follows: National Library of Wales (July

PERSONAL
PROPERTY

10, 1953, p. 452); National Library of Scotland (August 28, 1953, p. 555, and July 6, 1956, p. 416); Cambridge University Library (March 26, 1954, p. 207); the Bodleian Library (September 24, 1954, p. 616); Trinity College, Dublin (March 16, 1956, p. 172).

GUIDES TO LIBRARIES: Continental

La Bibliothèque Nationale

363 Catalogue générale des livres imprimés de la Bibliothèque nationale: Auteurs. Paris, 1897– .

364
365 ¶ For useful information on research libraries in various European countries, see MARGARET BURTON, Famous Libraries of the World (London, 1937); and ARUNDELL ESDAILE and F. J. HILL, National Libraries of the World (2nd ed., London, 1957).

BIBLIOGRAPHIES OF LITERATURE: English

370 For a comprehensive survey of modern bibliographical coverage of English literature, see ALEX PREMINGER, "English Literature," Library Trends, 15 (1966/7), 522–49.

371 LOWNDES, WILLIAM T.   The Bibliographer's Manual of English Literature.   New ed., by Henry G. Bohn.   6 vols.   London, 1857–64.

Z 2001 .L92

371a HARVARD UNIVERSITY LIBRARY. Widener Library Shelflist 35–38: English Literature.   4 vols.   Cambridge, Mass., 1971.

372 The New Cambridge Bibliography of English Literature, ed. George Watson.   5 vols.   Cambridge, 1969–77.   ("*NCBEL*")

ref Z 2011 -W32x

373 HOWARD-HILL, T. H.   Index to British Bibliography.   Vol. I: Bibliography of British Literary Bibliographies.   Oxford, 1969.

(ref) Z 2011 .H6

> For corrections and supplementary material, see Vol. II: Shakespearean Bibliography and Textual Criticism: A Bibliography (Oxford, 1971), pp. 179–322.

Roger Lund. Restoration & Early 18th-c. English Lit. 1660-1740: a Selected Bibliography of Resource Materials (MLA Series)

374 BESTERMAN, THEODORE. Literature English and American: A Bibliography of Bibliographies. Totowa, N.J., 1971.
> A reprint of the pertinent sections of **502**.

375 FINNERAN, RICHARD J. Anglo-Irish Literature: A Review of Research. New York, 1976.

Periods

378 ROBINSON, F. C. Old English Literature: A Select Bibliography. Toronto, 1970.

(handwritten: Z 2012 .R6)

379 ZESMER, DAVID M. Guide to English Literature from Beowulf through Chaucer and Medieval Drama. New York, 1961. *(handwritten: Eng. lang only acc. to Robinson)*

(handwritten: not at UWM)

380 FISHER, JOHN H. The Medieval Literature of Western Europe: A Review of Research, Mainly 1930–1960. New York, 1966.
> See Chapters 1–3.

381 WELLS, JOHN E. A Manual of the Writings in Middle English, 1050–1400. New Haven, 1916. Supplements. 9 vols. New Haven, 1919–52.
> Being superseded by J. BURKE SEVERS (later ALBERT E. HARTUNG), A Manual of the Writings in Middle English, 1050–1500 (New Haven, 1967–   ).

(handwritten: PR 255 .S4)

382 HAZLITT, W. CAREW. Hand-Book to the Popular, Poetical, and Dramatic Literature of Great Britain. London, 1867.
> Followed by various supplementary volumes, 1876–1903. The contents of most of these volumes are indexed in G. J. GRAY, A General Index to Hazlitt's Handbook and His Bibliographical Collections (London, 1893).

382a BOND, DONALD F. The Eighteenth Century. Northbrook, Ill., 1975.

382b BUCKLEY, J. H. Victorian Poets and Prose writers. 2nd ed. Arlington Heights, Ill., 1977.

383 TEMPLE, RUTH Z. Twentieth Century British Literature: A Reference Guide and Bibliography. New York, 1968.
> The author bibliographies are updated and supplemented in A Library of Literary Criticism: Modern British Literature, Volume IV: Supplement, ed. Martin Tucker and Rita Stein (New York, 1975).

383a LAUTERBACH, EDWARD S., and W. EUGENE DAVIS. The Transitional Age: British Literature 1880–1920. Troy, N.Y., 1973.

384 MELLOWN, ELGIN W. A Descriptive Catalogue of the Bibliographies of 20th Century British Writers. Troy, N.Y., 1972.

¶ All the foregoing must be supplemented by the appropriate serial bibliographies; see below, **452–464.**

Types

(A) POETRY

397 COLEMAN, ARTHUR. Epic and Romance Criticism. 2 vols. New York, 1973.

397a BEALE, WALTER H. Old and Middle English Poetry to 1500. Detroit, 1976.

398 BROWN, CARLETON. A Register of Middle English Religious and Didactic Verse. 2 vols. Oxford, 1916–20.
   Vol. II is superseded by the following item.

399 BROWN, CARLETON, and ROSSELL HOPE ROBBINS. The Index of Middle English Verse. New York, 1943.
   Supplement by R. H. ROBBINS and JOHN L. CUTLER (Lexington, Ky., 1965). 1st lines

   2012
   .B86

399a DYSON, A. E. English Poetry: Select Bibliographical Guides. Oxford, 1971.

400 JORDAN, FRANK. The English Romantic Poets. A Review of Research and Criticism. 3rd ed. New York, 1972.

   PR 590 .J6

401 HOUTCHENS, CAROLYN WASHBURN, and LAWRENCE HUSTON HOUTCHENS. The English Romantic Poets and Essayists: A Review of Research and Criticism. Revised ed. New York, 1966.

402 FAVERTY, FREDERIC E. The Victorian Poets: A Guide to Research. 2nd ed. Cambridge, Mass., 1968.

   PR 593 .F3

403 KUNTZ, JOSEPH M. Poetry Explication: A Checklist of Interpretation since 1925 of British and American Poems Past and Present. Revised ed. Denver, 1962.
   Supplemented by annual check lists of explications, printed in The Explicator, to which there is a two-volume cumulative index, covering Vols. 1–30.

(B) DRAMA

409 WELLS, STANLEY. English Drama (Excluding Shakespeare). London, 1975.

410 STRATMAN, CARL J. Bibliography of Medieval Drama. 2nd ed. 2 vols. New York, 1972.

411 ———. Bibliography of English Printed Tragedy, 1565–1900. Carbondale, Ill., 1966.

412 GREG, W. W. A Bibliography of the English Printed Drama to the Restoration. 4 vols. London, 1939–59.
Index of Characters by THOMAS L. BERGER and WILLIAM C. BRADFORD, JR. (Englewood, Colorado, 1975).

Z
2014
·D7

412a PENNINGER, FREIDA ELAINE. English Drama to 1660 (Excluding Shakespeare). Detroit, 1976.

413 WOODWARD, GERTRUDE L., and JAMES G. MCMANAWAY. A Check List of English Plays 1641–1700. Chicago, 1945.
Supplement by FREDSON BOWERS (Charlottesville, 1949).

Z
2014
.D7

413a LINK, FREDERICK M. English Drama, 1660–1800. Detroit, 1976.

413b CONOLLY, L. W., and J. P. WEARING. English Drama and Theatre, 1800–1900. Detroit, 1977.

413c MIKHAIL, E. H. English Drama, 1900–1950. Detroit, 1977.
Continued by the same author's Contemporary British Drama, 1950–1976 (Totowa, N.J., 1976).

414 BAKER, BLANCH M. Theatre and Allied Arts: A Guide to Books Dealing with the History, Criticism, and Technic of the Drama and Theatre and Related Arts and Crafts. New York, 1952.

415 COLEMAN, ARTHUR, and GARY R. TYLER. Drama Criticism: A Checklist of Interpretation Since 1940. 2 vols. Denver, 1966; Chicago, 1971.

416 ADELMAN, IRVING, and RITA DWORKIN. Modern Drama: A Checklist of Critical Literature on 20th-Century Plays. Metuchen, N.J., 1967.

¶ A wealth of bibliographical material concerning the English drama is also found in the standard histories and reference works mentioned above: YOUNG (**169**), CHAMBERS (**168, 171**), BENTLEY (**172**), and NICOLL (**173**).

(C) FICTION

418 WRIGHT, R. GLENN. Author Bibliography of English Language Fiction in the Library of Congress through 1950. 8 vols. Boston, 1973.

See also the same compiler's Chronological Bibliography of English Language Fiction with the same coverage (8 vols., Boston, 1974), and Title Bibliography (9 vols., Boston, 1976).

419 O'DELL, STERG. A Chronological List of Prose Fiction in English Printed in England and Other Countries 1475–1640. Cambridge, Mass., 1954.

420 MISH, CHARLES C. English Prose Fiction, 1600–1700. A Chronological Checklist. Charlottesville, 1967.

Z2014 F4 M6Y

421 McBURNEY, WILLIAM HARLIN. A Check List of English Prose Fiction 1700–39. Cambridge, Mass., 1960.

Z2014 F4 M33

421a BEASLEY, JERRY C. A Check List of Prose Fiction Published in England 1740–1749. Charlottesville, 1972.

Z2014 F4 B37

422 BLOCK, ANDREW. The English Novel, 1740–1850. A Catalogue Including Prose Romances, Short Stories, and Translations of Foreign Fiction. 2nd ed. London, 1961.

Z2014 F4 B6

Incomplete and unreliable. See *TLS*, April 21, 1961, p. 256; Robert A. Colby in Nineteenth-Century Fiction, 16 (1961/2), 354–59.

423 SADLEIR, MICHAEL. XIX Century Fiction: A Bibliographical Record Based on His Own Collection. 2 vols. Cambridge, 1951.

423a DYSON, A. E. The English Novel: Select Bibliographical Guides. London, 1974.

423b WATT, IAN. The British Novel: Scott through Hardy. Northbrook, Ill., 1973.

424 STEVENSON, LIONEL. Victorian Fiction: A Guide to Research. Cambridge, Mass., 1964.
   Supplemented by GEORGE H. FORD, Victorian Fiction: A Second Guide to Research (New York, 1978).

424a WILEY, PAUL L. The British Novel: Conrad to the Present. Northbrook, Ill., 1973.

425 BELL, INGLIS F., and DONALD BAIRD. The English Novel, 1578–1956: A Checklist of Twentieth-Century Criticisms. Denver, 1958.
   Supplemented by HELEN H. PALMER and JANE ANNE DYSON, English Novel Explication: Criticisms to 1972 (Hamden, Conn., 1973) and by PETER L. ABERNETHY et al., English Novel Explication Supplement 1 (Hamden, Conn., 1976).

425a BONHEIM, HELMUT, et al. The English Novel Before Richardson. A Checklist of Texts and Criticism to 1970. Metuchen, N.J., 1971.

425b ADELMAN, IRVING, and RITA DWORKIN. The Contemporary Novel: A Checklist of Critical Literature on the British and American Novel Since 1945. Metuchen, N.J., 1972.

425c DRESCHER, HORST, and BERND KAHRMANN. The Contemporary English Novel: An Annotated Bibliography of Secondary Sources. Frankfurt, 1973.

425d CASSIS, A. F. The Twentieth Century English Novel: An Annotated Bibliography of General Criticism. New York, 1977.

426 THURSTON, JARVIS, et al. Short Fiction Criticism: A Checklist of Interpretation since 1925 of Stories and Novelettes (American, British, Continental) 1800–1958. Denver, 1960.

427 WALKER, WARREN S. Twentieth-Century Short Story Explication: Interpretations, 1900–1975, of Short Fiction since 1800. 3rd ed. Hamden, Conn., 1977.

428 STALLMAN, ROBERT WOOSTER. "A Selected Bibliography of Criticism of Modern Fiction." Critiques and Essays on Modern Fiction 1920–1951, ed. John W. Aldridge (New York, 1952), pp. 553–610.

(D) PROSE

429 HENINGER, S. K., JR. English Prose, Prose Fiction, and Criticism to 1660. Detroit, 1975.

430 DE LAURA, DAVID J. Victorian Prose: A Guide to Research. New York, 1973.

(E) STYLISTICS

431 MILIC, LOUIS T. Style and Stylistics: An Analytical Bibliography. New York, 1967. ⟨≈⟩ *computer work*

432 BAILEY, RICHARD W., and DOLORES M. BURTON. English Stylistics: A Bibliography. Cambridge, Mass., 1968.

BIBLIOGRAPHIES OF LITERATURE: American

434 For a survey of modern bibliographical coverage of American literature, see JOHN T. FLANAGAN, "American Literary Bibliography in the Twentieth Century," Library Trends, 15 (1966/7), 550–72.

General

435 NILON, CHARLES H. Bibliography of Bibliographies in American Literature. New York, 1970.
Supplemented by PATRICIA PATE HAVLICE, Index to American Author Bibliographies (Metuchen, N.J., 1971).

436 GOHDES, CLARENCE. Bibliographical Guide to the Study of the Literature of the U.S.A. 4th ed. Durham, N.C., 1976.

437 SPILLER, ROBERT E., et al. Bibliography. Vol. II of Literary History of the United States (188).

438 LEARY, LEWIS, and JOHN AUCHARD. American Literature: A Study and Research Guide. New York, 1976.

439 KOLB, HAROLD H., JR. A Field Guide to the Study of American Literature. Charlottesville, Va., 1976.

440 CALLOW, JAMES T., and ROBERT J. REILLY. Guide to American Literature from Its Beginnings through Walt Whitman. New York, 1977.

441 CALLOW, JAMES T., and ROBERT J. REILLY. Guide to American Literature from Emily Dickinson to the Present. New York, 1977.

442 BLANCK, JACOB. Bibliography of American Literature. New Haven, 1955– .

Six volumes (HENRY ADAMS–THOMAS WILLIAM PARSONS) have appeared.

442a HARVARD UNIVERSITY LIBRARY. Widener Library Shelflist, 26: American Literature. 2 vols. Cambridge, Mass., 1970.

442b WOODRESS, JAMES. Eight American Authors: A Review of Research and Criticism. New York, 1972.

442c REES, ROBERT A., and EARL N. HARBERT. Fifteen American Authors Before 1900. Madison, 1971.

442d LEARY, LEWIS. Articles on American Literature [1900–1967]. ✗ 2 vols. Durham, N.C., 1954, 1970.

 3ʳᵈ vol out 1980
442e JONES, HOWARD MUMFORD, and RICHARD M. LUDWIG. Guide to American Literature and Its Background Since 1890. 4th ed. Cambridge, Mass., 1972.

442f BRYER, JACKSON R. Sixteen Modern American Authors: A Survey of Research and Criticism. Durham, N.C., 1974.

Types

(A) DRAMA

443 PALMER, HELEN H., and JANE ANNE DYSON. American Drama Criticism: Interpretations, 1890–1965. Hamden, Conn., 1967. Supplement I. Hamden, Conn., 1970. Supplement II, ed. Floyd Eugene Eddleman. Hamden, Conn., 1976.

See also COLEMAN and TYLER (**415**) and ADELMAN and DWORKIN (**416**).

(B) FICTION

445 WRIGHT, LYLE H. American Fiction 1774–1850: A Contribution toward a Bibliography. 2nd ed. San Marino, Cal., 1969.

Continued by the same author's American Fiction: 1851–1875 (San Marino, 1957) and by his American Fiction: 1876–1900 (San Marino, 1966).

All titles in these three volumes are being reproduced in microform.

See also WRIGHT (**418**) and TANSELLE (**779**), I, 83–86.

445a EICHELBERGER, CLAYTON L. A Guide to Critical Reviews of United States Fiction, 1870–1910. 2 vols. Metuchen, N.J., 1971–74.

446 GERSTENBERGER, DONNA, and GEORGE HENDRICK. The American Novel: A Checklist of Twentieth-Century Criticism on Novels Written Since 1789. 2 vols. Denver, 1961; Chicago, 1970.
See also ADELMAN and DWORKIN (**425b**), THURSTON (**426**), WALKER (**427**), and STALLMAN (**428**).

447 KIRBY, DAVID K. American Fiction to 1900. Detroit, 1975.

448 WOODRESS, JAMES. American Fiction 1900–1950. Detroit, 1974.

SERIAL BIBLIOGRAPHIES OF LITERATURE

For the years of the twentieth century prior to those covered by the various serial bibliographies, **685** (under earlier titles) is useful for finding scholarly articles in literature and related fields.

General

452 MODERN HUMANITIES RESEARCH ASSOCIATION. Annual Bibliography of English Language and Literature [1920–]. Cambridge, 1921– . ("MHRA Bibliography")

453 MLA International Bibliography of Books and Articles on the Modern Languages and Literatures. New York, 1922– .
Earlier titles: American Bibliography, Annual Bibliography.
Previous to issue for 1956, included books and articles by American scholars only. Until 1970 published as part of *PMLA*. Now published annually in separate fascicles, one of which is devoted to English and American literature.

454 ENGLISH ASSOCIATION. The Year's Work in English Studies [1919–]. London, 1921– . ("*YWES*")

455 Abstracts of English Studies. Boulder, Col., 1958– .

456 MLA Abstracts of Articles in Scholarly Journals. New York, 1971–75.

English: Periods

For the medieval period, see **481a, 482, 900a, 900b.**

459 "The Year's Work in Old English Studies [1967–]" and "Old English Bibliography [1969–]," both in Old English Newsletter, 1968– .ʊʊᴍ ᴅᴼᴇˢⁿᵗ ʰᵃᵛᵉ

460 "Literature of the Renaissance." Annually in *SP*, 1917–69. Coverage continued by MLA International Bibliography (**453**); for newly published books, see Quarterly Checklist of Renaissance Studies (**631**). On Shakespeare and related topics, see also "Shakespeare: An Annotated World Bibliography [1949–]," annually in Shakespeare Quarterly, 1950– , and "The Year's Contributions to Shakespearian Study" in Shakespeare Survey, 1948– .

461 "The Eighteenth Century: A Current Bibliography [1925–]." Annually in *PQ*, 1926–1975. Subsequently published by the American Society for Eighteenth-Century Studies. Issues for 1925–60 collected in Louis A. Landa et al., English Literature 1660–1800: A Bibliography of Modern Studies (6 vols., Princeton, 1950–72).   ✳

462 "The Romantic Movement: A Selective and Critical Bibliography [1936–]." Annually in *ELH*, 1937–49; *PQ*, 1950–64; and *ELN*, 1965– .

Collected in A. C. Elkins, Jr., and L. J. Forstner, The Romantic Movement Bibliography 1936–1970 (7 vols., Ann Arbor, 1973).

See also "Annual Bibliography [of Keats, Shelley, Byron, Hunt, etc., 1950–]," in Keats-Shelley Journal, 1952– . Collected in David B. Green and Edwin G. Wilson, Keats, Shelley, Byron, Hunt and Their Circles: A Bibliography, July 1, 1950–June 30, 1962 (Lincoln, Neb., 1964).

463 "Victorian Bibliography [1932–]." Annually in *MP*, 1933–57, and Victorian Studies, 1958– .

Issues for 1932–64 collected in William D. Templeman, Bibliographies of Studies in Victorian Literature for . . . 1932–1944 (Urbana, 1945); Austin Wright, Bibliographies of Studies in Victorian Literature for . . . 1945–1954 (Urbana, 1956); and Robert C. Slack, Bibliographies of Studies in Victorian Literature for . . . 1955–1964 (Urbana, 1967).

Z
2013
.B59

464 "Current Bibliography [of Twentieth-Century Literature, 1954–]." Quarterly in Twentieth-Century Literature (**644**), 1955– .

> Collected, with many additions, in DAVID E. POWNALL, Articles on Twentieth Century Literature: An Annotated Bibliography 1954 to 1970 (7 vols., New York, 1973–76).

> See also the Annual Review Number of the Journal of Modern Literature (**619**).

> ¶ In addition, Studies in English Literature (**638**) contains valuable annual surveys of scholarship: English Renaissance (in the winter issue), Elizabethan and Jacobean Drama (spring), Restoration and Eighteenth Century (summer), Nineteenth Century (autumn).

American

471 "Articles on American Literature Appearing in Current Periodicals [1929–]." Quarterly in *AL*, 1929– .

> All materials appearing in this bibliography through 1967 are gathered in LEARY (**438**).

472 "Articles in American Studies [1954–72]." Annually in American Quarterly, 1955–73.

> Collected in HENNIG COHEN, Articles in American Studies 1954–1968 (2 vols., Ann Arbor, 1972).

473 American Literary Scholarship: An Annual [1963–]. Durham, N.C., 1965– .

Special Topics

480 "Annual Bibliography [on Style, 1966–]." Style, 1967– .

481 "A Selective Check List of Bibliographical Scholarship [1949–74]." Annually in Studies in Bibliography, 1950/1–1975.

> Issues for 1949–55 gathered, with index, in Studies in Bibliography, 10 (1957). Issues for 1956–62 gathered, with index, in Selective Check Lists of Bibliographical Scholarship, Series B (Charlottesville, 1966). Supplemented and then supplanted by the annual bibliography in Proof: The Yearbook of American Bibliographical and Textual Studies, 1971– .

Z
6203
· R66

481a ROUSE, RICHARD H.   Serial Bibliographies for Medieval Studies.   Berkeley, 1969.
    See also **900a** and **900b**.

482 "A Bibliography of Critical Arthurian Literature [1936–62]." Annually in *MLQ*, 1940–63.
    Preceded by JOHN J. PARRY and MARGARET SCHLAUCH, A Bibliography of Critical Arthurian Literature for [1922–35] (2 vols., New York, 1931–36). Now superseded by Bibliographical Bulletin of the International Arthurian Society, 1949– .

483 "Annual Bibliography [of Comparative Literature, 1949–69]." In Yearbook of Comparative and General Literature, 1952–70.
    Supplements FERNAND BALDENSPERGER and WERNER P. FRIEDRICH, Bibliography of Comparative Literature (Chapel Hill, 1950).

484 Bibliographie générale de littérature comparée [1949–58]. Paris, 1950–58.

485 "Anglo-German Literary Bibliography [1933–70]."   Annually in *JEGP*, 1935–71.

486 "Selective Current Bibliography for Aesthetics and Related Fields [1945–72]."   Annually in Journal of Aesthetics and Art Criticism, 1945/6–73.

487 "Annual Bibliography of Folklore [1887–64]." Journal of American Folklore, 1888–1963; Abstracts of Folklore Studies, 1964–65.

488 "Folklore Bibliography [1937–   ]."   Annually in Southern Folklore Quarterly, 1938–   .

489 "Modern Drama: A Selective Bibliography of Works Published in English in [1959–   ]."   Annually in Modern Drama, 1960–   .
    Suspended 1969–74, subsequently resumed.

490 "Annual Bibliography of Short Fiction Interpretation."   Studies in Short Fiction, 1964–   .

491 An Index to Book Reviews in the Humanities.   Detroit, 1960–   .

492 Book Review Index.   Detroit, 1965–   .

(IND)

cumulative

Nat'l Libr. Service *Bk Rv. Index* $\frac{Z}{1035}$ – 1980   Z
(Princeton)   .A1   1035

New Yk Times Bk Review Index   .A1
           B6

GENERAL REFERENCE GUIDES

494 MALCLÈS, LOUISE-NOËLLE. Les Sources du travail bibliographique. 3 vols. in 4. Geneva, 1950–58.

495 SHEEHY, EUGENE P. Guide to Reference Books. 9th ed. Chicago, 1976.

496 DOWNS, ROBERT B. How to Do Library Research. Urbana, 1966.

497 WALFORD, A. J. Guide to Reference Material. 3rd ed. 3 vols. 1973–77.
Volume III lists works on literature and the arts.

BIBLIOGRAPHIES OF BIBLIOGRAPHIES

502 BESTERMAN, THEODORE. A World Bibliography of Bibliographies. 4th ed. 5 vols. Lausanne, 1965–66.

503 COURTNEY, WILLIAM P. A Register of National Bibliography. 3 vols. London, 1905–12.

504 Bibliographic Index: A Cumulative Bibliography of Bibliographies [1937–   ]. New York, 1938–   .

505 ¶ On books of this class, as well as of the three following classes, see ROBERT L. COLLISON, Bibliographies: Subject and National (3rd ed., New York, 1968). See also HOWARD-HILL (**373**) for bibliographies of literary bibliographies.

UNIVERSAL BIBLIOGRAPHIES

511 WATT, ROBERT. Bibliotheca Britannica; or a General Index to British and Foreign Literature. 4 vols. Edinburgh, 1824.

512 GRÄSSE, JOHANN GEORG THEODOR. Trésor de livres rares et précieux. 7 vols. Dresden, 1859–69.

513 BRUNET, JACQUES CHARLES. Manuel du libraire et de l'amateur de livres. 6 vols. Paris, 1860–65. Supplement. 2 vols. Paris, 1878–80.
Additional volume (1870): Dictionnaire de géographie ancienne et moderne.

AUTHOR BIBLIOGRAPHIES

See Howard-Hill (373), Sheehy (495), Walford (497), Bibliographic Index (504), Collison (505), and Tanselle (779), as well as many of the items listed under Bibliographies of Literature and Serial Bibliographies of Literature.

SUBJECT CATALOGUES

519 British Museum. Subject Index of Modern Books Acquired [1881–]. London, 1902– .
Title varies.

520 Peddie, R. A. Subject Index of Books Published before 1880. 4 vols. London, 1933–48.
Complementary to 519.

521 Subject-Index of the London Library. 4 vols. London, 1909–55.

522 Library of Congress Catalog: Books: Subjects [1950–]. Ann Arbor, 1955; Washington, 1956– .

523 Subject Guide to Books in Print. New York, 1957– .
For the work to which this is a subject index, see Publishers' Trade List Annual (812).

¶ For further subject-indexing, see the British Museum General Catalogue (338) (for authors as subjects), the printed catalogues of individual American and British libraries, the Cumulative Book Index (810), the American Book Publishing Record (813), British Books in Print (790), the English Catalogue (787), Whitaker's Cumulative Book List (788), and the British National Bibliography (789). For subject-indexing of periodicals, see 680–89. See also the indexes to the Bulletin of the New York Public Library (655), a periodical which has often printed valuable subject bibliographies.

INDEXES TO COMPOSITE BOOKS

529 The "A.L.A." Index: An Index to General Literature. 2nd ed. Boston, 1901. Supplement, 1900–10. Chicago, 1914.
(*Entry continued on next page.*)

Indexed in C. EDWARD WALL, A.L.A. Index to General Literature: Cumulative Author Index (Ann Arbor, 1972).

Indexing of composite books was continued in the Readers' Guide (**684**) to 1914.

530 Essay and General Literature Index, 1900–33. New York, 1934. Supplementary volumes. New York, 1941– .

GUIDES TO ANONYMOUS AND PSEUDONYMOUS LITERATURE

536 HALKETT, SAMUEL, and JOHN LAING. Dictionary of Anonymous and Pseudonymous English Literature. New ed. 9 vols. Edinburgh, 1926–62.

¶ For further help in identifying the authors of anonymous
537 and pseudonymous works, see ARCHER TAYLOR and FREDERIC J. MOSHER, The Bibliographical History of Anonyma and Pseudonyma (Chicago, 1951). The 1948 Supplement to the LC Catalog (**313**) identifies the authors of "approximately 26,000 anonymous and pseudonymous" works. For identification of authors of articles in 19th-century English periodicals, see the Wellesley Index (**681**). See also HAROLD S. SHARP, Handbook of Pseudonyms and Personal Nicknames (2 vols., Metuchen, N.J., 1972), together with its supplement (2 vols., 1975).

ENCYCLOPEDIAS

542 The New Encyclopaedia Britannica. 15th ed. 30 vols. Chicago, 1974.

543 Enciclopedia Italiana. 35 vols. and index. Rome, 1929–39. Supplements 1–3. Rome, 1938–61.

544 La Grande Encyclopédie. 31 vols. Paris, 1886–1902.
A totally new work, under the same title, was issued in 20 volumes, 1971–76.

545 New Catholic Encyclopedia. 15 vols. New York, 1967.

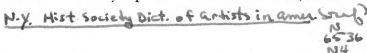

N.Y. Hist. Society Dict. of artists in amer. sup?
N
6536
N4

Music
also   Macmillan _Ency_. of Music & Musicians

546 The Century Dictionary and Cyclopedia. 12 vols. New York, 1911.

A new edition of the Cyclopedia of Names was published in 1954.

547 Encyclopaedia of Religion and Ethics, ed. James Hastings. 13 vols. New York, 1908–27.

548 Encyclopaedia of the Social Sciences, ed. Edwin R. A. Seligman and Alvin Johnson. 15 vols. New York, 1930–35.

549 A Dictionary of the Social Sciences, ed. Julius Gould and William L. Kolb. New York, 1964.

550 International Encyclopedia of the Social Sciences. 17 vols. New York, 1968.

551 Grove's Dictionary of Music and Musicians, ed. Eric Blom. 5th ed. 9 vols. London, 1954. Supplement. London, 1961.

552 Encyclopedia Judaica. 16 vols. Jerusalem, 1971–72.

553 The Encyclopedia of Philosophy, ed. Paul Edwards. 8 vols. New York, 1967.

Reprinted in four volumes, 1973.

554 Dictionary of the History of Ideas: Studies of Selected Pivotal Ideas, ed. Philip P. Wiener. 4 vols. New York, 1973. Index, 1974.

¶ For comments on these encyclopedias, as well as the titles of numerous others in various fields of interest, see SHEEHY (**495**) and WALFORD (**497**).

DICTIONARIES

English

557 A New English Dictionary on Historical Principles, ed. James A. H. Murray et al. 10 vols. in 15. Oxford, 1888–1928.

(*"NED"* or *"OED"*)

The "corrected reissue," with supplement, is called The Oxford English Dictionary (13 vols., Oxford, 1933).

A three-volume Supplement is being issued. The first volume, A–G, appeared in 1972; the second, H–N, in 1976.

558 The Shorter Oxford English Dictionary, ed. William Little et al. 3rd ed. Oxford, 1955.

559 The American Heritage Dictionary of the English Language, ed. William Morris. Boston, 1969.
The best recent dictionary, recording English and American usages.

560 FOWLER, H. W. A Dictionary of Modern English Usage. 2nd ed., revised by Sir Ernest Gowers. Oxford, 1965.

561 PARTRIDGE, ERIC. A Dictionary of Slang and Unconventional English. 7th ed. 2 vols. London, 1970.

American

566 A Dictionary of American English on Historical Principles, ed. William Craigie and James R. Hulbert. 4 vols. Chicago, 1938–44.   (*"DAE"*)

567 A Dictionary of Americanisms, ed. Mitford M. Mathews. 2 vols. Chicago, 1951.

568 NICHOLSON, MARGARET. A Dictionary of American-English Usage. New York, 1957.
Based on the first edition of FOWLER (**560**).

569 FOLLETT, WILSON, et al. Modern American Usage. New York, 1966.

570 WENTWORTH, HAROLD, and STUART BERG FLEXNER. Dictionary of American Slang. "Second supplemented edition." New York, 1975.

Greek

574 A Greek-English Lexicon, ed. Henry George Liddell and Robert Scott. Revised ed. Oxford, 1940.

Latin

580 LEWIS, CHARLTON T., and CHARLES SHORT. A Latin Dictionary. Oxford, 1962.

581 Cassell's New Latin-English, English-Latin Dictionary, ed. D. P. Simpson. London, 1959.

French

587 Harrap's New Standard French and English Dictionary, ed.
J. E. Mansion, revised by R. P. L. and Margaret Ledésert. 2
vols. New York, 1972.
Volumes I and II are French-English. The English-French
volume of the former edition (1940) has not yet been revised.

588 The New Cassell's French Dictionary, ed. Denis Girard et al.
New York, 1962.

German

594 Langenscheidt's New Muret-Sanders Encyclopedic Diction-
ary of the English and German Languages, ed. Otto Springer.
Part I: English-German. 2 vols. New York, 1962–63. Part
II: German-English. 2 vols. Berlin, 1974–75.

595 Cassell's German and English Dictionary, ed. Harold T. Bet-
teridge. London, 1957.

Spanish

597 A New Pronouncing Dictionary of the Spanish and English
Languages, ed. Mariano Velázquez de la Cadena. Revised
ed. by Edward Gray and Juan L. Iribas. New York, 1967.

598 Cassell's Spanish Dictionary: Spanish-English, English-Span-
ish, ed. Allison Peers et al. London, 1959.

SCHOLARLY PERIODICALS

A list limited to journals most often consulted by scholars in
English and American literature.   For the full range of periodicals that have some bearing on literary studies, see the
list prefixed to the MLA International Bibliography (**453**);

601 DONNA GERSTENBERGER and GEORGE HENDRICK, Fourth Directory of Periodicals Publishing Articles on English and
American Literature and Language.   Chicago, 1974; WILLIAM
602 PELL, "Facts of Scholarly Publishing," *PMLA*, 88 (1973), es-
603 pecially pp. 644–54; and GARY L. HARMON and SUSANNA M.
HARMON, Scholar's Market: An International Directory of
Periodicals Publishing Literary Scholarship (Columbus, Ohio,
1974).

Literature

605 American Literary Realism, 1870–1910. 1967– .
Cumulative index, Vols. 1–10, in Vol. 10.

606 American Literature. 1929/30– . (*"AL"*)
Indexed in THOMAS F. MARSHALL, An Analytical Index to American Literature Volumes 1–30, March 1929–January 1959 (Durham, N.C., 1963).

607 Anglia. 1877– .
Cumulative indexes to Vols. 1–50, 51–75.

608 The Chaucer Review: A Journal of Medieval Studies and Literary Criticism. 1966– .

609 Early American Literature. 1966– .

610 Eighteenth-Century Studies. 1967– .

611 ELH. 1934– .

612 Emerson Society Quarterly: A Journal of the American Renaissance. 1955– .

613 English Language Notes. 1963– . (*"ELN"*)

614 English Literary Renaissance. 1972– .

615 English Literature in Transition 1880–1920. 1957– .
Title 1957–62: English Fiction in Transition. Cumulative Index, Vols. 1–15.

616 English Studies [Amsterdam]. 1919– .
Cumulative index, Vols. 1–40.

617 Études Anglaises. 1937– .

618 JEGP: Journal of English and Germanic Philology. 1897– .
Cumulative index to Vols. 1–50 printed as a supplement to Vol. 61, No. 4 (1962).

619 Journal of Modern Literature. 1970– .

620 Keats-Shelley Journal. 1952– .
Cumulative index, Vols. 1–9, in Vol. 10.

620a Literary Research Newsletter. 1976– .

621 Modern Fiction Studies. 1955– .

622 Modern Language Quarterly. 1940– .   *("MLQ")*

623 Modern Language Review. 1905/6– .   *("MLR")*
    Cumulative indexes to Vols. 1–10, 11–20, 21–30, 31–50, 51–60.

624 Modern Philology. 1903/4– .   *("MP")*

625 New Literary History: A Journal of Theory and Interpretation. 1969– .

626 Nineteenth-Century Fiction. 1945– .
    Title 1945–49: The Trollopian. Cumulative index, Vols. 1–30.

627 Novel: A Forum on Fiction. 1967– .
    Cumulative index, Vols. 1–5.

628 Papers on Language and Literature. 1965– .
    Title of Vol. 1: Papers on English Language and Literature.
    Cumulative index to Vols. 1–6 in Vol. 6.

629 Philological Quarterly. 1922– .   *("PQ")*
    Cumulative index to Vols. 1–25.

630 PMLA: Publications of the Modern Language Association of America. 1884/5– .
    Cumulative indexes to Vols. 1–50, 51–60, 61–79.

631 Quarterly Checklist of Renaissance Studies. 1959– .
    Merged with Quarterly Checklist of Medievalia, 1976.

632 Renaissance Drama. 1955– .
    Title 1955–63: Research Opportunities in Renaissance Drama.

633 Renaissance Quarterly. 1948– .
    Title 1948–66: Renaissance News.

634 Resources for American Literary Study. 1971– .

635 The Review of English Studies. 1925– .   *("RES")*

636 Shakespeare Quarterly. 1950– .
    Cumulative index, Vols. 1–15.

637 Shakespeare Survey. 1948– .
    Published annually. Cumulative indexes, Vols. 1–10, 11–20, in Vols. 10 and 21, respectively.

638 Studies in English Literature 1500–1900. 1961– .

639 Studies in Philology. 1906– .   (*"SP"*)
    Cumulative index to Vols. 1–50.

640 Studies in Scottish Literature. 1963– .

641 Studies in Short Fiction. 1963– .
    Cumulative index, Vols. 1–10, in Vol. 12.

642 Studies in the Novel. 1969– .

643 Texas Studies in Literature and Language. 1958– .

644 Twentieth Century Literature: A Scholarly and Critical Journal. 1955– .

645 Victorian Poetry. 1963– .

¶ In addition, there are many informal organs of specialized groups which contain useful articles, notes, reviews, etc.; for example, the Wordsworth Circle, the Johnsonian News Letter, the Thoreau Society Bulletin, the Walt Whitman Review, the Shavian, Conradiana, the Virginia Woolf Newsletter.

Analytical Bibliography, History of Printing, etc.

647 The Library. 1889– .
    Merged in 1920 with the Transactions of the Bibliographical Society, begun in 1893. Indexed in GEORGE W. COLE, An Index to Bibliographical Papers Published by the Bibliographical Society and the Library Association, London, 1877–1932 (Chicago, 1933).

648 Papers of the Bibliographical Society of America. 1904/5– .
                                          (*"PBSA"*)
    Cumulative indexes to Vols. 1–25, 26–45.

649 Studies in Bibliography. Papers of the Bibliographical Society of the University of Virginia. 1948/9– .   (*"SB"*)
    Published annually.

650 Proof: The Yearbook of American Bibliographical and Textual Studies. 1971– .

651 ABHB: Annual Bibliography of the History of the Printed Book and Libraries. 1970– .

¶ See G. THOMAS TANSELLE, "The Periodical Literature of English and American Bibliography," *SB*, 26 (1973), 167–91.

Publications of Research Libraries

653 Harvard Library Bulletin. 1947–60; 1967– .
Cumulative indexes to Vols. 1–10, 11–14.

654 The Huntington Library Quarterly. 1937/8– .
Preceded by Huntington Library Bulletin, 1931–37.

655 Bulletin of the New York Public Library. 1897– .
Continued by Bulletin of Research in the Humanities, 1978– .
Cumulative indexes to Vols. 1–40, 41–50, 51–66.

Allied Fields

660 American Speech. 1925/6– .

661 Comparative Literature. 1949– .
Cumulative index to Vols. 1–15.

662 Comparative Literature Studies. 1964– .

663 Journal of Aesthetics and Art Criticism. 1941– .

664 Journal of American Folklore. 1888– .
Cumulative index to Vols. 1–70.

665 Journal of the History of Ideas. 1940– .   (*"JHI"*)

666 The New England Quarterly. 1928– .
Cumulative index to Vols. 1–10.

667 Speculum. 1926– .

668 Studies in Romanticism. 1961– .
Preceded by Boston University Studies in English, 1955–61.

668a Studies in the Renaissance. 1954– .

668b Studies in the Twentieth Century. 1968– .

669 Victorian Studies. 1957– .
Cumulative index to Vols. 1–20.

Little Magazines

See HOFFMAN, The Little Magazine (**720**).

General

673 TLS: The [London] Times Literary Supplement. 1902– .

674   Notes and Queries. 1849/50– .   (*"N&Q"*)
      Fifteen cumulative indexes through 1947.

675   American Notes & Queries. 1962– .

GENERAL PERIODICALS AND NEWSPAPERS

Indexes to Periodicals

680   Poole's Index to Periodical Literature, 1802–81. Revised ed.
      Boston, 1891. Supplements, 1882–1907. 5 vols. Boston,
      1887–1908.

      Indexed by author in C. EDWARD WALL, Cumulative Author
      Index for Poole's Index to Periodical Literature 1802–1906
      (Ann Arbor, 1971).

      Use with MARION V. BELL and JEAN C. BACON, Poole's Index
      Date and Volume Key (Chicago, 1957), which supersedes the
      "Chronological Conspectus" of the original Poole volumes.

      VINTON A. DEARING, Transfer Vectors for Poole's Index to
      Periodical Literature (Los Angeles, 1967), expands and identi-
      fies Poole's abbreviations, and correlates volumes and years.

680a Literary Writings in America: A Bibliography. 8 vols. Mill-
      wood, N.Y., 1977.

681   The Wellesley Index to Victorian Periodicals, 1824–1900, ed.
      Walter E. Houghton et al. Toronto, 1966– .
      To be completed in four volumes.

682   Nineteenth Century Readers' Guide to Periodical Literature,
      1890–99. 2 vols. New York, 1944.

683   The Magazine Subject-Index: A Subject-Index to Seventy-
      Nine American and English Periodicals. 2 vols. Boston,
      1908.

      Continued by Annual Magazine Subject-Index [1909–49] (Bos-
      ton, 1910–52). Complete file gathered in Cumulated Maga-
      zine Subject-Index 1907–1949 (2 vols., Boston, 1964).

684   Readers' Guide to Periodical Literature [1900–]. Minne-
      apolis (later New York), 1901– .

685   Humanities Index. New York, 1916– .
      Earlier titles: Readers' Guide Supplement, International Index
      to Periodicals, Social Sciences and Humanities Index. Cov-
      erage began with 1907.

686 British Humanities Index. London, 1916– .
Title 1916–61: Subject Index to Periodicals.

686a The American Humanities Index. 1975– .

687 Index to Little Magazines [1948–]. Denver (later Troy, N.Y.), 1949– .
Six retrospective volumes, covering the years 1900–47, were published 1965–74. Title varies.

688 An Author Index to Selected British "Little Magazines" 1930–39, ed. B. C. Bloomfield. London, 1976.

689 Comprehensive Index to English-Language Little Magazines 1890–1970. Series One, ed. Marion Sader. 8 vols. Millwood, N.Y., 1976.

Indexes to Newspapers

(I ND)

693 The New York Times Index [1913–]. New York, 1913– . A I
Prior Series, covering 1851–1912 (New York, 1966–). 21
, N44

694 Palmer's Index to the [London] Times Newspaper [1790–1941]. London, 1868–1943.

(REF)
AI

695 Index to the [London] Times [1906–]. London, 1907– . 21
Title varies. Times mF A N O4 T46

Bibliographies and Location Guides

703 Union List of Serials in Libraries of the United States and Canada, ed. Edna Brown Titus. 3rd ed. 5 vols. New York, 1965. *("ULS")*
Supplemented by New Serial Titles (Washington, 1950–). Issues for 1950–70 cumulated in 3 volumes. (Washington, 1973).

For a bibliography of union lists of serials for various geographical regions, see RUTH S. FREITAG, Union Lists of Serials: A Bibliography (Washington, 1964).

704 British Union-Catalogue of Periodicals. 4 vols. London, 1955–58. Supplement. London, 1962.
Supplements issued quarterly and cumulated annually.
Issues for 1960–73 cumulated in two volumes (London, 1970, 1976).

705 Union Catalogue of the Periodical Publications in the University Libraries of the British Isles, ed. Marion G. Roupell. London, 1937.

706 BRITISH MUSEUM. Periodical Publications [Vols. 184–186 of the General Catalogue of Printed Books (338)].

707 [MUDDIMAN, J. G.] The Times Tercentenary Handlist of English and Welsh Newspapers, Magazines and Reviews [1620–1920]. London, 1920.
To be used with caution. See corrections in *N&Q*, 1921–22.

708 BRITISH MUSEUM. Newspapers Published in Great Britain and Ireland, 1801–1900. London, 1905.

708a The Waterloo Directory of Victorian Periodicals 1824–1900. Phase 1. Waterloo, Ontario, 1976.

709 BRIGHAM, CLARENCE S. History and Bibliography of American Newspapers 1690–1820. 2 vols. Worcester, Mass., 1947.
Additions and corrections in Proceedings of the American Antiquarian Society, 71 (1961), 15–62. *Includes locations*

See also EDWARD CONNERY LATHEM, Chronological Tables of American Newspapers 1620–1820 (Barre, Mass., 1972).

710 American Newspapers 1821–1936: A Union List of Files Available in the United States and Canada, ed. Winifred Gregory. New York, 1937.
See also TANSELLE (779), I, 135–37.

711 CRANE, RONALD S., and F. B. KAYE. A Census of British Newspapers and Periodicals 1620–1800. Chapel Hill, 1927.
Originally published in *SP*, 24 (1927), 1–205.
Supplemented by:

GABLER, ANTHONY J. "Check-List of English Newspapers and Periodicals before 1801 in the Huntington Library." Huntington Library Bulletin, No. 2 (1931), 1–66.

MILFORD, R. T., and D. M. SUTHERLAND. A Catalogue of English Newspapers and Periodicals in the Bodleian Library, 1622–1800. Oxford Bibliographical Society Proceedings and Papers, 4 (1934/5), 163–346.

(*Entry continued on next page.*)

[handwritten annotation:] Brit. Newspapers & Period. : 1641-1700 : A Short Title Cat. ... Ed. Carolyn W. Nelson & Matt. Seccombe. MLA, 1988.

STEWART, POWELL. British Newspapers and Periodicals 1632–1800 [in the University of Texas Library]. Austin, 1950.

WILES, R. M. Freshest Advices: Early Provincial Newspapers in England. Columbus, Ohio, 1965.
See Appendix C: "Register of English Provincial Newspapers, 1701–1760."

712 WARD, WILLIAM S. Index and Finding List of Serials Published in the British Isles, 1789–1832. Lexington, Ky., 1953.

713 WEED, KATHERINE KIRTLEY, and RICHMOND P. BOND. Studies of British Newspapers and Periodicals from Their Beginning to 1800: A Bibliography. *SP*, extra series, No. 2 (1946).

714 WARD, WILLIAM S. British Periodicals and Newspapers, 1789–1832: A Bibliography of Secondary Sources. Lexington, Ky., 1972.

715 MADDEN, LIONEL, and DIANA DIXON. The Nineteenth-Century Periodical Press in Britain: A Bibliography of Modern Studies, 1901–1971. New York, 1975.

716 WHITE, ROBERT B., JR. The English Literary Journal to 1900. Detroit, 1977.

716a KRIBBS, JAYNE K. An Annotated Bibliography of American Literary Periodicals, 1741–1850. Boston, 1977.

717 CHIELENS, EDWARD E. The Literary Journal in America to 1900. Detroit, 1975.

717a ———. The Literary Journal in America, 1900–1950. Detroit, 1977.

¶ For extensive lists of British newspapers and magazines, and studies thereof, see the *NCBEL* (**372**), II, cols. 1257–1390, III, cols. 1755–1884, and IV, cols. 1329–1408.

---

718 LIBRARY OF CONGRESS. Newspapers in Microform. 2 vols. Washington, 1973.
See also Guide to Microforms in Print (**830**).

719 MOTT, FRANK LUTHER. A History of American Magazines [1741–1930]. 5 vols. New York (later Cambridge, Mass.), 1930–68.

720 HOFFMAN, FREDERICK J., et al. The Little Magazine: A History and a Bibliography. Princeton, 1946.
See also Union List of Little Magazines [in the libraries of six midwestern universities] (Chicago, 1956).

720a HAMILTON, IAN. The Little Magazines. London, 1976.

721 Ulrich's International Periodicals Directory. New York, 1932– .
Published biennially.

722 Irregular Serials and Annuals: An International Directory. New York, 1967– .
Published biennially.

¶ Extensive files of English and American periodicals, 18th–20th centuries, are now available in many libraries on microfilm.

AIDS FOR TRACING PARTICULAR COPIES OF BOOKS
Guides to Book Collectors

727 DE RICCI, SEYMOUR. English Collectors of Books and Manuscripts (1530–1930). New York, 1930.

728 CANNON, CARL L. American Book Collectors and Collecting. New York, 1941.

¶ For a list of printed catalogues of some great collections formerly in private hands see KENNEDY, Concise Bibliography (14), 3rd ed., pp. 24–27. Catalogues of the personal libraries of a number of English authors are reproduced in facsimile
729 in A. N. L. MUNBY, Sale Catalogues of Libraries of Eminent Persons. 12 vols. (London, 1971–75).

Bibliographies of Book-Sale Catalogues

734 BRITISH MUSEUM. List of Catalogues of English Book Sales, 1676–1900, Now in the British Museum. London, 1915.

734a MUNBY, A. N. L., and LENORE CORAL. British Book Sale Catalogues 1676–1800. London, 1977.
Supplements but does not supersede the foregoing, with enlarged coverage for the period indicated.

735 MCKAY, GEORGE L. American Book Auction Catalogues 1713–1934: A Union List. New York, 1937.
Additions in the Bulletin of the New York Public Library, 50 (1946), 177–84; 52 (1948), 401–12.

Current Book-Auction Records

741 Book-Prices Current: A Record of Prices at Which Books Have Been Sold at Auction. London, 1888–1957.
Three cumulative indexes, covering the years 1887–1916.
Not at uwm

742 Book-Auction Records: A Priced and Annotated Annual Record of London, New York, Montreal, Edinburgh, and Glasgow Book Auctions [1902–]. London, 1903– .
Eight cumulative indexes, covering the years 1902–73.

743 American Book-Prices Current. New York, 1895– .
Ten cumulative indexes, covering the years 1916–75.

744 United States Cumulative Book Auction Records. New York, 1940–51. Not at uwm

ANALYTICAL BIBLIOGRAPHY

750 BOWERS, FREDSON. "Bibliography, Pure Bibliography, and Literary Studies." *PBSA,* 46 (1952), 186–208.

751 WILSON, F. P. Shakespeare and the New Bibliography. Revised by Helen Gardner. Oxford, 1970.

752 GASKELL, PHILIP. A New Introduction to Bibliography. Oxford, 1972.
Intended to supersede the classic Introduction to Bibliography for Literary Students by RONALD B. MCKERROW (Oxford, 1927).

753 BOWERS, FREDSON. Principles of Bibliographical Description. Princeton, 1949.

754 ALDIS, HARRY G. The Printed Book. 3rd ed., revised by John Carter and Brooke Crutchley. Cambridge, 1951.

755 Esdaile's Manual of Bibliography. 4th ed., revised by Roy Stokes. London, 1967.

756 BRIQUET, CHARLES M. Les Filigranes [1282–1600]. 2nd ed. 4 vols. Leipzig, 1923.
The "facsimile edition" (Amsterdam, 1968) contains valuable additional material in Vol. I.
Supplemented by W. A. CHURCHILL, Watermarks in Paper in Holland, England, France, etc., in the Seventeenth and Eighteenth Centuries (Amsterdam, 1935) and by EDWARD HEAWOOD, Watermarks: Mainly of the 17th and 18th Centuries (Hilversum, 1950).

BOOK-TRADE HISTORY

English

763 PLANT, MARJORIE. The English Book Trade: An Economic History of the Making and Sale of Books. 3rd ed. London, 1974.

764 CLAIR, COLIN. A History of Printing in Britain. London, 1965.

765 MUMBY, FRANK ARTHUR, and IAN NORRIE. Publishing and Bookselling. 5th ed. London, 1974.

766 DUFF, EDWARD G. A Century of the English Book Trade [1457–1557]. London, 1905.
Continued by the following five works:

767 ——, et al. Hand Lists of English Printers, 1501–1556. 4 parts. London, 1895–1913. *includes identifying marks*

768 McKERROW, R. B. A Dictionary of Printers and Booksellers in England, Scotland and Ireland . . . 1557–1640. London, 1910.

769 PLOMER, HENRY R. A Dictionary of the Booksellers and Printers . . . in England, Scotland and Ireland from 1641 to 1667. London, 1907.

770 ———, et al. A Dictionary of the Printers and Booksellers . . . from 1668 to 1725. London, 1922.

771 ———, et al. A Dictionary of the Printers and Booksellers . . . from 1726 to 1775. London, 1932.

772 MAXTED, IAN. The London Book Trades 1775–1800: A Preliminary Checklist of Members. London, 1977.

¶ See also Morrison's indexes (**795, 796**) of printers, publishers, and booksellers in *STC* and Wing.

American

778 LEHMANN-HAUPT, HELLMUT, et al. The Book in America. 2nd ed. New York, 1951.
The original edition (1939) contains sections deleted from the later edition.

779 TANSELLE, G. THOMAS. Guide to the Study of United States Imprints. 2 vols. Cambridge, Mass., 1971.

780 TEBBEL, JOHN. A History of Book Publishing in the United States. 3 vols. New York, 1972– .

¶ See also Bristol's index (**822**) of printers, publishers, and booksellers in Evans.

NATIONAL BIBLIOGRAPHIES: English

Contemporary Lists

784 ARBER, EDWARD. A Transcript of the Registers of the Company of Stationers of London, 1554–1640. 5 vols. London, 1875–77; Birmingham, 1894.   ("Stationers' Register")
To be used with W. W. GREG, A Companion to Arber (Oxford, 1967).

785 [EYRE, G. E. B.] A Transcript of the Registers of the Worshipful Company of Stationers from 1640–1708. 3 vols. London, 1913–14.

786 ARBER, EDWARD. The Term Catalogues, 1668–1709. A Contemporary Bibliography of English Literature in the Reigns of Charles II, James II, William and Mary, and Anne. 3 vols. London, 1903–06.

786a Foxon, D. F.   English Bibliographical Sources.   1964–   .
    1. The Monthly Catalogue 1714–17.   London, 1964.
    2. The Monthly Catalogue 1723–30.   2 vols.   London, 1964.
    3. A Register of Books 1728–32.   London, 1964.
    4. Bibliotheca Annua 1699–1703.   2 vols.   London, 1964.
    5. The Annual Catalogue 1736–37.   London, 1965.
    6. The Gentleman's Magazine 1731–51.   London, 1966.
    7. The Monthly Catalogues from The London Magazine 1732–66.   London, 1966.
    8. The Lists of Books from The British Magazine 1746–50. London, 1965.

Series II, Catalogues of English Printed Books (London, 1965–66), reprints similar lists of "books in circulation" in 1595 and 1657–95.

787   The English Catalogue of Books [1801–1970].   London, 1864–1970.
The period 1801–36 is covered in a retrospective volume, ed. Robert Alexander Peddie and Quintin Waddington (London, 1914).   From 1837 onward, a contemporary list, published annually and then cumulated into larger volumes at varying intervals.   Basis of the list is the bimonthly one appearing in The Publisher, successor to the Publishers' Circular (1837–1959) and British Books (1959–70).

788   Whitaker's Cumulative Book List.   London, 1924–   .
Quarterly and annual cumulations of lists published weekly and monthly in The Bookseller and monthly in Current Literature.

789   The British National Bibliography.   London, 1950–   .
Published weekly; cumulated quarterly and annually.   Cumulated indexes and subject catalogues published every five years.

790   British Books in Print.   London, 1874–   .
Title 1874–1965: The Reference Catalogue of Current Literature.

791   Paperbacks in Print.   London, 1960–   .

(815)   Guide to Reprints.   Washington, 1967–   .

¶ See also Cumulative Book Index (810).

Retrospective Lists

795   Pollard, A. W., and G. R. Redgrave.   A Short-Title Catalogue of Books Printed in England, Scotland, and Ireland, and of English Books Printed Abroad, 1475–1640.   London, 1926.
("*STC*")

(Entry continued on next page.)

Vol. III P to Z 1641-1700
2nd ed. Donald Wing MLA 1988

Indexed in PAUL G. MORRISON, Index of Printers, Publishers, and Booksellers in [the Short-Title Catalogue] (Charlottesville, 1950), and in A. F. ALLISON and V. F. GOLDSMITH, Titles . . . Volume I, 1475–1640 (Hamden, Conn., 1976). See also WILLIAM WARNER BISHOP, A Checklist of American Copies of "Short-Title Catalogue" Books (2nd ed., Ann Arbor, 1950), and DAVID RAMAGE, A Finding-List of English Books to 1640 in Libraries in the British Isles (Durham, 1958).

Volume II of the second edition appeared in 1976; Volume I is forthcoming.

All titles listed in the *STC* are being made available on microform.

extension of Pollard & Redgrave

796 WING, DONALD. Short-Title Catalogue of Books Printed in England, Scotland, Ireland, Wales, and British America and of English Books Printed in Other Countries, 1641–1700. 3 vols. New York, 1945–51.

2nd ed. 2002

Indexed in PAUL G. MORRISON, Index of Printers, Publishers and Booksellers [in Wing] (Charlottesville, 1955), and in A. F. ALLISON and V. F. GOLDSMITH, Titles . . . Volume II, 1641–1700 (Hamden, Conn., 1977). See also Supplement in Huntington Library Quarterly, 16 (1953), 393–436; and J. E. ALDEN, Wing Addenda & Corrigenda (Charlottesville, 1958); and WING, A Gallery of Ghosts: Books Published between 1641–1700 Not Found in the Short-Title Catalogue (New York, 1967).

Volume I of the second edition appeared in 1972. Volumes II and III are forthcoming.

A large selection of the works listed in Wing is being made available on microform.

797 FOXON, D. F. English Verse 1701–1750: A Catalogue of Separately Printed Poems. 2 vols. Cambridge, 1975.

NATIONAL BIBLIOGRAPHIES: American

Contemporary Lists

807 ROORBACH, O. A. Bibliotheca Americana. Catalogue of American Publications 1820–[1861]. 4 vols. New York, 1852–61.

As the dates indicate, these volumes are partly retrospective.

808 The American Catalogue of Books [1861–71]. 2 vols. New York, 1866–71.

809 The American Catalogue of Books [1876–1910]. 13 vols. New York, 1880–1911.

810 Cumulative Book Index [1898–]. Minneapolis (later New York), 1900– . ("*CBI*")
"A World List of Books in the English Language."

811 Publishers'Weekly. New York, 1872– .
Weekly lists of newly published books.

812 The Publishers' Trade List Annual [1873–]. New York, 1874– .
Indexed in <u>Books in Print</u>: An Author-Title-Series Index to the Publishers' Trade List Annual (New York, 1948–) and in Subject Guide to Books in Print (523).

(CAT)
Z
1215
.P97

813 American Book Publishing Record. New York, 1960– .

814 Paperbound Books in Print. New York, 1955– .

815 Guide to Reprints. Washington, 1967– .

Retrospective Lists

821 SABIN, JOSEPH. Bibliotheca Americana: A Dictionary of Books Relating to America, from its Discovery to the Present Time. 29 vols. New York, 1868–1936.
Indexed in JOHN EDGAR MOLNAR, Author-Title Index to Joseph Sabin's Dictionary of Books Relating to America (3 vols., Metuchen, N.J., 1974).

For important information about the successive reductions of scope during the long process of compilation, see introduction to Vol. XXIX. (Since the contents are not limited to books published in America this is not, strictly speaking, a national bibliography.) *all titles are microfilmed*

The New Sabin, ed. Laurence S. Thompson, began to be issued in 1974.

822 EVANS, CHARLES. American Bibliography: A Chronological Dictionary of All Books, Pamphlets and Periodical Publications Printed in the United States of America from the Gene-
all entries are on microfilm (*Entry continued on next page.*)

sis of Printing in 1639 down to and Including the Year 1820.
13 vols. and index. Chicago (later Worcester, Mass.), 1903–
59. Supplement by Roger P. Bristol. Charlottesville, 1970.
Reaches only through 1800. Indexed in R. P. BRISTOL, Index
of Printers, Publishers, and Booksellers [in Evans] (Charlottesville, 1961), and Index to Supplement to Charles Evans' American Bibliography (Charlottesville, 1971). See also the National Index of American Imprints through 1800: the Short-Title
Evans, ed. CLIFFORD K. SHIPTON and JAMES E. MOONEY (2
vols., [Worcester, Mass.], 1970).

All titles listed in Evans are being made available in microprint.

823 SHAW, RALPH R., and RICHARD H. SHOEMAKER. American
Bibliography: A Preliminary Checklist [1801–19]. 20 vols.
New York, 1958–65. *all entries on microfilm*
Supplements: Title Index, 1965; Corrections and Author Index,
1966. All titles listed are being microfilmed.

824 SHOEMAKER, RICHARD H., et al. A Checklist of American Imprints for [1820–   ]. Metuchen, N.J., 1964–   .

NATIONAL BIBLIOGRAPHIES: Other Nations

For annotated lists of the older and currently appearing national bibliographies of European and South American countries, see SHEEHY (**495**), MALCLÈS (**494**), and HELEN F.
828 CONOVER, Current National Bibliographies (Washington,
1955).

MICROFORMS

830 Guide to Microforms in Print. Washington, 1961–   .

831 National Register of Microform Masters. Washington,
1965–   .

832 VEANER, ALLEN B., and ALAN M. MECKLER. International
Microforms in Print: A Guide to Microforms of Non-United
States Micropublishers. Weston, Conn., 1974–   .
Supplements but does not duplicate **830**, which is confined to
U.S. micropublishers.

832a Micropublishers' Trade List Annual. London, 1975–   .

GUIDES TO DISSERTATIONS

833 REYNOLDS, MICHAEL M. A Guide to Theses and Dissertations: An Annotated International Bibliography of Bibliographies. New York, 1975.

834 Comprehensive Dissertation Index 1861–1972. 37 vols. Ann Arbor, 1973. Supplements [1973–]. 1974– .

837 Dissertation Abstracts International. Ann Arbor, 1938– .
Title 1938–51: Microfilm Abstracts; 1951–69: Dissertation Abstracts. Beginning with Vol. 27 (1966), divided into two series: (A) Humanities and Social Sciences; (B) Sciences.

Vols. 1–29 (1938–69) indexed in Retrospective Index (9 vols., 1970); see Vol. 8 for dissertations on literature.

838 Retrospective Index to Theses of Great Britain and Ireland, 1716–1950. Volume I: Social Science and Humanities. Oxford, 1975.
Continued by Index to Theses Accepted for Higher Degrees in the Universities of Great Britain and Ireland [1950/1–] (London, 1953–).

839 McNAMEE, LAWRENCE F. Dissertations in English and American Literature: Theses Accepted by American, British and German Universities, 1865–1964. New York, 1968. Supplement One, 1964–68. New York, 1969. Supplement Two, 1969–73. New York, 1974.

840 MUMMENDEY, RICHARD. Language and Literature of the Anglo-Saxon Nations as Presented in German Doctoral Dissertations 1885–1950. Charlottesville, 1954.
Seriously incomplete.

841 ALTICK, RICHARD D., and WILLIAM R. MATTHEWS. Guide to Dissertations in Victorian Literature 1886–1958. Urbana, 1960.

842 WOODRESS, JAMES. Dissertations in American Literature, 1891–1966. 3rd ed. Durham, N.C., 1968.
Continued by list of completed dissertations in each issue of American Literature (606), which also contains a record of dissertations in progress.

PALEOGRAPHY

844 THOMPSON, SIR EDWARD MAUNDE. "The History of English Handwriting, A.D. 700–1400." Transactions of the Bibliographical Society, 5 (1898–1900), 109–42, 213–53.
See also his article, "Handwriting," in Shakespeare's England (959), I, 284–310.

845 JENKINSON, HILARY. "Elizabethan Handwritings: A Preliminary Sketch." The Library, 4th ser., 3 (1922), 1–34.

846 BYRNE, MURIEL ST. CLARE. "Elizabethan Handwriting for Beginners." RES, 1 (1925), 198–209.

847 HECTOR, L. C. The Handwriting of English Documents. 2nd ed. London, 1966.

848 DAWSON, GILES E., and LAETITIA KENNEDY-SKIPTON. Elizabethan Handwriting, 1500–1650: A Manual. New York, 1966.

MANUSCRIPTS

Catalogues of Manuscripts

850 RICHARDSON, ERNEST CUSHING. A List of Printed Catalogs of Manuscript Books. (Part 3 of A Union World Catalog of Manuscript Books.) New York, 1935.
"Indispensable but uncritical and full of errors" (Paul Kristeller).

851 KRISTELLER, PAUL OSKAR. Latin Manuscript Books Before 1600: A List of the Printed Catalogues and Unpublished Inventories of Extant Collections. 3rd ed. New York, 1965.
Has broader usefulness than the title indicates.

852 BRITISH MUSEUM. Catalogue of Additions to the Manuscripts. London, 1843– .
Title varies. Retrospective to 1783. Far in arrears. For announcements of important recent accessions, see the British Museum Quarterly (1926–).

(340) SKEAT, T. C. "The Catalogues of the British Museum. 2. Manuscripts." Journal of Documentation, 7 (1951), 18–60.
Revised edition (London, 1962).

Bodleian Quarterly

Z,
662/
.096

853 HUNT, R. W., et al.   A Summary Catalogue of Western Manuscripts in the Bodleian Library at Oxford.   7 vols. in 8.   Oxford, 1895–1953.

854 OWEN, A. E. B.   Summary Guide to Accessions of Western Manuscripts (Other than Medieval) since 1867 [in the Cambridge University Library].   Cambridge, 1966.

855 KER, NEIL R.   Medieval Manuscripts in British Libraries. Oxford, 1969– .
> To be completed in three volumes.

856 HISTORICAL MANUSCRIPTS COMMISSION.   A Guide to the Reports on Collections of Manuscripts of Private Families, Corporations and Institutions in Great Britain and Ireland.   2 vols. in 3.   London, 1914–38.
> Supplemented by Guide to the Reports . . . 1911–1957, Part 1: Index of Places, ed. A. S. C. HALL (London, 1973) and Part 2: Index of Persons, ed. A. S. C. HALL (3 vols., London, 1966).

> See convenient guide to these reports in MULLINS, Texts and Calendars (**920**), Chapter 7.

857 CRICK, B. R., and MIRIAM ALMAN.   A Guide to Manuscripts Relating to America in Great Britain and Ireland.   London, 1961.

858 DE RICCI, SEYMOUR, and W. J. WILSON.   Census of Medieval and Renaissance Manuscripts in the United States and Canada.   3 vols.   New York, 1935–40.   Supplement by W. H. Bond.   New York, 1962.

859 ROBBINS, J. ALBERT, et al.   American Literary Manuscripts: A Checklist of Holdings in Academic, Historical, and Public Libraries, Museums and Authors' Homes in the United States. 2nd ed.   Athens, Ga., 1977.

860 HAMER, PHILIP M.   A Guide to Archives and Manuscripts in the United States.   New Haven, 1961.

Ref
Z
6620
.U5
N3

861 The National Union Catalog of Manuscript Collections [1959–].   Ann Arbor (later Hamden, Conn., etc.), 1962– .
> Cumulative indexes are issued at intervals of three or four years.

862 SCHULZ, HERBERT C. "American Literary Manuscripts in the Huntington Library," Huntington Library Quarterly, 22 (1959), 209–50, and "English Literary Manuscripts in the Huntington Library," ibid., 31 (1968), 251–302.

862a Catalog of Manuscripts of the Folger Shakespeare Library, Washington, D.C. 3 vols. ˉBoston, 1971.

¶ For good lists of the catalogues of manuscripts at the English universities and other British libraries, see DOWNS, British Library Resources (**327**). For printed guides to American collections, see DOWNS, American Library Resources (**287**).

Using and Editing Manuscripts; Textual Criticism

(The term "textual criticism" applies not only to manuscripts but to printed texts as well.)

863 BOWERS, FREDSON. "Textual Criticism and the Literary Critic." Textual and Literary Criticism (Cambridge, 1959), pp. 1–34.

864 [KENNEY, E. J.] "Textual Criticism." Encyclopaedia Britannica, 1974.

865 THORPE, JAMES. Principles of Textual Criticism. San Marino, Cal., 1972.

865a DEARING, VINTON A. Principles and Practice of Textual Analysis. Berkeley, 1974.

865b THORPE, JAMES. The Use of Manuscripts in Literary Research. New York, 1974.

866 BRACK, O. M., JR., and WARNER BARNES, eds. Bibliography and Textual Criticism: English and American Literature 1700 to the Present. Chicago, 1969.

867 GOTTLSMAN, RONALD, and SCOTT BENNETT, eds. Art and Error: Modern Textual Editing. Bloomington, 1970.

868 IVY, G. S. "The Bibliography of the Manuscript-Book," in Francis Wormald and C. E. Wright, eds., The English Library before 1700 (London, 1958), pp. 32–65.

PUBLIC RECORDS

871 GALBRAITH, V. H. An Introduction to the Use of the [British] Public Records. Oxford, 1934.
See also GALBRAITH's Studies in the Public Records (London, 1948), Chapter 1.

872 Guide to the Contents of the Public Record Office. 3 vols. London, 1963–68.

873 ¶ See the article by HILARY JENKINSON in the first edition of Raymond Irwin, ed., The Libraries of London (London, 1949), pp. 55–91, for additional and more recent information on the Public Record Office. This description may use-
874 fully be supplemented by The British Public Record Office (Richmond, Va., 1960) [Virginia Colonial Records Project, Special Reports 25, 26, 27].

For the Calendars of State Papers (Domestic and Foreign) and related calendars of English public records from the middle ages onwards—now totaling upwards of six hundred volumes—see the convenient list in MULLINS, Text and Calendars (**920**), pp. 16–36.

875 Guide to the National Archives of the United States. Washington, 1974.

HISTORY: General

Handbooks and Encyclopedias

879 LANGER, WILLIAM L. An Encyclopedia of World History. 5th ed. Boston, 1972.

880 MORRIS, RICHARD B., and GRAHAM W. IRWIN. Harper Encyclopedia of the Modern World: A Concise Reference History from 1760 to the Present. New York, 1970.

881 KELLER, HELEN REX. The Dictionary of Dates. 2 vols. New York, 1934.

882 Haydn's Dictionary of Dates and Universal Information Relating to All Ages and Nations, ed. Benjamin Vincent. 25th ed. New York, 1911.
First published 1841. Contents vary with each edition.

883 LITTLE, CHARLES E. Cyclopedia of Classified Dates. New York, 1899.

883a Everyman's Dictionary of Dates, ed. Audrey Butler. 6th ed. New York, 1971.

884 MAYER, ALFRED. Annals of European Civilization 1501–1900. London, 1949.

884a GRUN, BERNARD. The Timetables of History: A Horizontal Linkage of People and Events. New York, 1975.

884b STOREY, R. L. Chronology of the Medieval World 800–1491. London, 1973.

885 WILLIAMS, NEVILLE. Chronology of the Expanding World, 1492–1762. London, 1969.

886 ———. Chronology of the Modern World, 1763 to the Present Time. 3rd ed. London, 1975.

Histories

890 The Cambridge Medieval History, ed. H. M. Gwatkin et al. 8 vols. Cambridge, 1911–36.

891 The Cambridge Modern History, ed. A. W. Ward et al. 13 vols. Cambridge, 1902–11.
Now supplanted in part by the following work.

892 The New Cambridge Modern History, ed. G. R. Potter et al. 12 vols. and atlas. Cambridge, 1957–70.
Issued without bibliographies: but JOHN ROACH, A Bibliography of Modern History (Cambridge, 1968), supplements the bibliographies in **891**.

Bibliographies

899 DUTCHER, GEORGE MATTHEW, et al. A Guide to Historical Literature. New York, 1931.

900 International Bibliography of Historical Sciences [1926–]. Washington (later Paris, etc.), 1930– .
No volumes for 1940–46. The gap is partly filled by LOUIS B. FREWER, Bibliography of Historical Writings Published in Great Britain and the Empire, 1940–45 (Oxford, 1947).

See also JOAN C. LANCASTER, Bibliography of Historical Works Issued in the United Kingdom, 1946–1956 (London, 1957), and three volumes by WILLIAM KELLAWAY, Bibliography of Historical Works Issued in the United Kingdom [1957–70] (London, 1962, 1967, 1972).

900a International Guide to Medieval Studies: A Quarterly Index to Periodical Literature. Darien, Conn., 1961– .

900b International Medieval Bibliography. Minneapolis, 1967– .

901 The American Historical Association's Guide to Historical Literature, ed. George Frederick Howe et al. New York, 1961.

HISTORY: English

Handbooks

908 POWICKE, SIR F. MAURICE, and E. B. FRYDE, eds. Handbook of British Chronology. 2nd ed. London, 1961.

909 HAYDN, JOSEPH, and HORACE OCKERBY. The Book of Dignities, Containing Lists of the Official Personages of the British Empire. 3rd ed. London, 1894.

910 STEINBERG, S. H., and I. H. EVANS. Steinberg's Dictionary of British History. 2nd ed. London, 1970.

Histories

915 The Oxford History of England. Oxford, 1934–65.
    I.   R. G. COLLINGWOOD and J. N. L. MYRES. Roman Britain and the English Settlements. 2nd ed. 1937.
    II. F. M. STENTON. Anglo-Saxon England, c. 550–1087. 3rd ed. 1971:
    III. A. L. POOLE. From Domesday Book to Magna Carta, 1087–1216. 2nd ed. 1955.
    IV. SIR MAURICE POWICKE. The Thirteenth Century, 1216–1307. 2nd ed. 1962.
    V. MAY McKISACK. The Fourteenth Century, 1307–99. 1959.
    VI. ERNEST F. JACOB. The Fifteenth Century, 1399–1485. 1961.
    VII. J. D. MACKIE. The Earlier Tudors, 1485–1558. 1952.

(*Entry continued on next page*)

   VIII. J. B. BLACK. The Reign of Elizabeth, 1558–1603. 2nd ed. 1959.

     IX. GODFREY DAVIES. The Early Stuarts, 1603–60. 2nd ed. 1959.

      X. G. N. CLARK. The Later Stuarts, 1660–1714. 2nd ed. 1956.

    XI. BASIL WILLIAMS. The Whig Supremacy, 1714–60. 2nd ed., revised by C. H. Stuart. 1962.

   XII. J. STEVEN WATSON. The Reign of George III, 1760–1815. 1960.

  XIII. SIR LLEWELLYN WOODWARD. The Age of Reform, 1815–70. 2nd ed. 1962.

  XIV. R. C. K. ENSOR. England, 1870–1914. 1936.

   XV. A. J. P. TAYLOR. English History, 1914–1945. 1965.

Bibliographies

919 MULLINS, E. L. C. A Guide to the Historical and Archaeological Publications of Societies in England and Wales, 1901–1933. London, 1968.

920 ————. Texts and Calendars: An Analytical Guide to Serial Publications. London, 1958.

921 GRAVES, EDGAR B. A Bibliography of English History to 1485. Oxford, 1975.

921a GRANSDEN, ANTONIA. Historical Writing in England c.550–c.1307. Ithaca, N.Y., 1974.

922 BONSER, WILFRID. An Anglo-Saxon and Celtic Bibliography (450–1087). 2 vols. Berkeley, 1957.

923 ALTSCHUL, MICHAEL. Anglo-Norman England 1066–1154. Cambridge, 1969.

923a GUTH, DELLOYD J. Late Medieval England 1377–1485. Cambridge, 1976.

924 READ, CONYERS. Bibliography of British History: Tudor Period, 1485–1603. 2nd ed. Oxford, 1959.
    Supplemented by MORTIMER LEVINE, Tudor England, 1485–1603 (Cambridge, 1968).

925 DAVIES, GODFREY. Bibliography of British History: Stuart Period 1603–1714. 2nd ed., revised by Mary Frear Keeler. Oxford, 1970.

925a SACHSE, WILLIAM L. Restoration England 1660–1689. Cambridge, 1971.

926 PARGELLIS, STANLEY, and D. J. MEDLEY. Bibliography of British History: The Eighteenth Century, 1714–1789. Oxford, 1951.

926a BROWN, LUCY M., and IAN R. CHRISTIE. Bibliography of British History 1789–1851. Oxford, 1977.

927 ALTHOLZ, JOSEF L. Victorian England 1837–1901. Cambridge, 1970.

927a HANHAM, H. J. Bibliography of British History 1851–1914. Oxford, 1976.

927b HAVIGHURST, ALFRED F. Modern England 1901–1970. Cambridge, 1976.

928 ROYAL HISTORICAL SOCIETY. Writings on British History 1901–1933. A Bibliography of Books and Articles on the History of Great Britain from about 400 A.D. to 1914. 5 vols. in 7. London, 1968–70.
> Coverage extended by the serial Writings on British History [1934–] (London, 1937–), the latest volume of which (1973) carries the record through 1948. For publications on British history issued in the United Kingdom since that date, see LANCASTER and KELLAWAY (900).

929 ROYAL HISTORICAL SOCIETY. Annual Bibliography of British and Irish History [1975–]. Atlantic Highlands, N.J., 1976– .

HISTORY: American

Handbooks and Encyclopedias

933 ADAMS, JAMES TRUSLOW, and R. V. COLEMAN. Dictionary of American History. 7 vols. New York, 1976.
> An index volume is forthcoming.

934 Concise Dictionary of American History, ed. Wayne Andrews. New York, 1962.

935 MORRIS, RICHARD B., and JEFFREY B. MORRIS. Encyclopedia of American History. Bicentennial ed. New York, 1976.

936 The Oxford Companion to American History, ed. Thomas H. Johnson. New York, 1966.

Histories

939 HOFSTADTER, RICHARD, et al. The United States: the History of a Republic. 2nd ed. Englewood Cliffs, N.J., 1967.

940 MORISON, SAMUEL ELIOT, et al. The Growth of the American Republic. 6th ed. 2 vols. New York, 1969.

941 WILLIAMS, T. HARRY, et al. A History of the United States. 3rd ed. 2 vols. New York, 1969.

Bibliographies

946 BEERS, HENRY PUTNEY. Bibliographies in American History. Revised ed. New York, 1942.

947 FREIDEL, FRANK. Harvard Guide to American History. Revised ed. 2 vols. Cambridge, Mass., 1974.

948 BASLER, ROY P., et al. A Guide to the Study of the United States of America. Washington, 1960. Supplement 1956–65. Washington, 1976.

949 Writings on American History [1902–   ]. Princeton (later Washington), 1904–   .
Volumes for 1904–05 and 1941–47 were never published. Cumulative index, 1902–40.

To be concluded with volume for 1961. The subsequent decade is covered by Writings on American History 1962–73: A Subject Bibliography of Articles (4 vols., Washington, 1976). The earlier serial is now replaced by Writings on American History 1973–74 [et seq.]: A Subject Bibliography of Articles (1974–   ).

950 America: History and Life. A Guide to Periodical Literature. Santa Barbara, 1964–   .

SOCIAL HISTORY

English

955 TRAILL, H. D., ed. Social England. 6 vols. London, 1893–97. Illustrated ed. 6 vols. London, 1901–04.

956 TREVELYAN, G. M. English Social History. London, 1942. Also issued, with a wealth of illustrations, as Illustrated English Social History (4 vols., London, 1949–52).

957 COULTON, G. G. Medieval Panorama. Cambridge, 1938.

958 POOLE, AUSTIN LANE, ed. Medieval England. 2nd ed. 2 vols. Oxford, 1958.

959 [ONIONS, C. T., et al., eds.] Shakespeare's England. 2 vols. Oxford, 1916.

960 TURBERVILLE, A. S., ed. Johnson's England. 2 vols. Oxford, 1933.

961 [YOUNG, G. M., ed.] Early Victorian England, 1830–65. 2 vols. London, 1934.

962 NOWELL-SMITH, SIMON, ed. Edwardian England, 1901–1914. London, 1964.

American

967 SCHLESINGER, ARTHUR M., and DIXON R. Fox, eds. A History of American Life. 13 vols. New York, 1927–48.

968 FURNAS, J. C. The Americans: A Social History of the United States 1587–1914. New York, 1969.

BIOGRAPHY

General

970 Biographie universelle ancienne et moderne. Nouvelle éd. 45 vols. Paris, 1843–65.

972 HYAMSON, ALBERT M. A Dictionary of Universal Biography of All Ages and of All Peoples. 2nd ed. London, 1951.

973 SLOCUM, ROBERT B. Biographical Dictionaries and Related Works. Detroit, 1967. Supplement. Detroit, 1972.

974 Biography Index: A Cumulative Index to Biographical Material in Books and Magazines [1946–]. New York, 1947– .

975 Contemporary Authors: A Bio-Bibliographical Guide to Current Authors and Their Works, ed. James M. Ethridge et al. Detroit, 1963– .
Cumulative index to Vols. 1–20 in BARBARA HARTE and CAROLYN RILEY, 200 Contemporary Authors (Detroit, 1969).

975a Contemporary Poets, ed. James Vinson and D. L. Kirkpatrick. 2nd ed. London, 1975.

975b Contemporary Novelists, ed. James Vinson. 2nd ed. New York, 1976.

975c Contemporary Dramatists, ed. James Vinson. New York, 1973.

975d Contemporary Literary Critics, ed. Elmer Borklund. London, 1977.

976 Chambers's Biographical Dictionary, ed. J. O. Thorne. Revised ed. New York, 1969.

English

977 Dictionary of National Biography, ed. Leslie Stephen and Sidney Lee. 63 vols. London, 1885–1900. (Later reprinted in 21 vols.)   ("*DNB*")
[First] Supplement (3 vols., London, 1901).

Errata (London, 1904). (For later corrections of *DNB* information see Corrections and Additions to the Dictionary of National Biography Cumulated from the Bulletin of the Institute of Historical Research, University of London [Boston, 1966].)

Second Supplement (3 vols., London, 1912) and succeeding decennial volumes (1927–71) contain articles on eminent persons who died 1900–60. The 1951–60 supplement includes an index to the whole series.

The Compact Edition (2 vols., Oxford, 1975)—which includes all the supplementary and decennial volumes through 1960—contains a single general index of great usefulness.

See important articles in *TLS*, December 24, 1971, pp. 1593–95, and November 3, 1973, p. 1314.

978 The Dictionary of National Biography: The Concise Dictionary. Part 1 . . . to 1900. Oxford, 1953. Part 2: 1901–1950. Oxford, 1961.

979 BOASE, FREDERICK. Modern English Biography, Containing Many Thousand Concise Memoirs of Persons Who Have Died Since the Year 1850. 3 vols. Truro, etc., 1892–1901. Supplement. 3 vols. Truro, etc., 1908–21.

980 C[OKAYNE], G. E. The Complete Peerage of England, Scotland, Ireland, Great Britain and the United Kingdom, Extant, Extinct, or Dormant. New ed. 14 vols. London, 1910–59.

981 ———. Complete Baronetage. 5 vols. and index. Exeter, 1900–09.

982 Burke's . . . Landed Gentry, ed. Peter Townend. 18th ed. 3 vols. London, 1965–72.

983 Alumni Cantabrigienses: A Biographical List . . . from the Earliest Times to 1900, ed. John Venn and J. A. Venn. 10 vols. Cambridge, 1922–54.

984 Alumni Oxonienses: The Members of the University of Oxford [1500–1886], ed. Joseph Foster. 8 vols. London, 1887–92.

985 MATTHEWS, WILLIAM. British Diaries: An Annotated Bibliography of British Diaries Written between 1442 and 1942. Berkeley, 1950.
   Supplemented by JOHN STUART BATTS, British Manuscript Diaries of the Nineteenth Century: An Annotated Listing (Totowa, N.J., 1976).

986 ———. British Autobiographies: An Annotated Bibliography of British Autobiographies Published or Written Before 1951. Berkeley, 1955.

¶ ALLIBONE'S DICTIONARY (39) contains biographical information on thousands of minor literary figures. For valuable information on the genealogical aspects of biographical re-
987 search relating to English figures, see ANTHONY RICHARD WAGNER, English Genealogy (2nd ed., Oxford, 1972), Chapters 8–10.

American

990 Dictionary of American Biography, ed. Allen Johnson and Dumas Malone. 20 vols. and index. New York, 1928–37. Five supplements. New York, 1944–77.   (*"DAB"*)
The supplements bring the record down to December 31, 1955.

991 Concise Dictionary of American Biography. 2nd ed. New York, 1977.

992 KAPLAN, LOUIS. A Bibliography of American Autobiographies. Madison, 1961.

993 MATTHEWS, WILLIAM. American Diaries: An Annotated Bibliography of American Diaries Written Prior to the Year 1861. Berkeley, 1945.
Supplemented by the same author's American Diaries in Manuscript, 1580–1954: A Descriptive Bibliography (Athens, Ga., 1974).

994 DARGAN, MARION. Guide to American Biography. 2 vols. in 1. Albuquerque, 1949–52.

995 Appletons' Cyclopaedia of American Biography. 7 vols. New York, 1886–1900.
Subsequently reprinted with excisions, 1915. Five supplementary volumes issued 1918–31.

To be used with caution; contains an undetermined number of ghost biographies. See MARGARET C. SCHINDLER, "Fictitious Biography," American Historical Review, 42 (1937), 680–90.

Some Books Every Student of Literature Should Read

In certain sections of this handbook, notably those on literary and cultural and intellectual history, are listed a number of works, like Matthiessen's *American Renaissance* and Lovejoy's *The Great Chain of Being*, which every student of literature should not merely refer to, but read. Here is a further selection of books, not so easily classifiable, the reading of which should be a part of one's education in modern tendencies in criticism, aesthetics, the history and theory of literature, and the history of ideas. Needless to say, the list is a sampling, and further titles will occur to every observer of contemporary literary thought.

AUERBACH, ERICH. Mimesis: The Representation of Reality in Western Literature. Princeton, 1953.
BOOTH, WAYNE C. The Rhetoric of Fiction. Chicago, 1961. ✔
BLOOM, HAROLD. The Anxiety of Influence: A Theory of Poetry. New York, 1973.
BURKE, KENNETH. The Philosophy of Literary Form. Baton Rouge, 1941.
CULLER, JONATHAN. Structuralist Poetics: Structuralism, Linguistics, and the Study of Literature. Ithaca, N.Y., 1975.
ELIOT, T. S. Selected Essays. 3rd ed. London, 1951.
EMPSON, WILLIAM. Seven Types of Ambiguity. 3rd ed. London, 1953.
FEIDELSON, CHARLES, JR. Symbolism and American Literature. Chicago, 1953.
FERGUSSON, FRANCIS. The Idea of a Theater. Princeton, 1949.
FISH, STANLEY. Self-Consuming Artifacts. Berkeley, 1972.
✓FORSTER, E. M. Aspects of the Novel. New York, 1927.

145

✓ FRYE, NORTHROP. Anatomy of Criticism. Princeton, 1957.

GARDNER, HELEN. The Business of Criticism. London, 1959.

HARTMAN, GEOFFREY H. The Fate of Reading. Chicago, 1975.

HOLLOWAY, JOHN. The Victorian Sage: Studies in Argument. London, 1953.

JAMESON, FREDRIC. The Prison-House of Language: A Critical Account of Structuralism and Russian Formalism. Princeton, 1972.

KRIEGER, MURRAY. Theory of Criticism. Baltimore, 1976.

LANGER, SUSANNE K. Philosophy in a New Key. Cambridge, Mass., 1942.

LEAVIS, F. R. The Common Pursuit. London, 1952.

LEVIN, HARRY. Contexts of Criticism. Cambridge, Mass., 1957.

LOWES, JOHN LIVINGSTON. The Road to Xanadu: A Study in the Ways of the Imagination. Revised ed. Boston, 1930.

✓ LUBBOCK, PERCY. The Craft of Fiction. London, 1921.

MARTZ, LOUIS L. The Poetry of Meditation: A Study in English Religious Literature of the Seventeenth Century. New Haven, 1954.

ORWELL, GEORGE. Shooting an Elephant. London, 1950.

RICHARDS, I. A. Principles of Literary Criticism. 5th ed. New York, 1934.

SMITH, HENRY NASH. Virgin Land: The American West as Symbol and Myth. Cambridge, Mass., 1950.

SPITZER, LEO. Linguistics and Literary History: Essays in Stylistics. Princeton, 1948.

TRILLING, LIONEL. The Liberal Imagination: Essays on Literature and Society. New York, 1950.

TUVE, ROSEMOND. Elizabethan and Metaphysical Imagery. Chicago, 1947.

WILLIAMS, RAYMOND. Culture and Society 1780–1950. London, 1958.

WILLIAMSON, GEORGE. The Senecan Amble: A Study in Prose Form from Bacon to Collier. London, 1951.

WILSON, EDMUND. Axel's Castle: A Study in the Imaginative Literature of 1870–1930. New York, 1948.

A Glossary of Useful Terms

For further discussion of many of the terms found here, and of many more not included in this list, see Geoffrey Ashall Glaister, *An Encyclopedia of the Book* (New York, 1960) and John Carter, *ABC for Book Collectors* (5th ed., London, 1972), as well as books on analytical bibliography (**752–755**) and on historical method (**23–27, 947**).

A.L.S. Autograph letter, signed; a letter wholly in the handwriting of its author. *L.S.* means a letter signed by its author but otherwise written by somebody else. *T.L.S.*—not to be confused with *TLS* (**673**)—means "typed letter, signed."

accidentals In textual editing, "the written form of all words . . . spelling, capitalization, word-division, and punctuation . . . as distinguished from . . . 'substantives,' or the forms of words as distinguished from the words themselves" (Fredson Bowers).

analytical bibliography The branch of scholarship which, by examining such evidence as that provided by types, signatures, watermarks, and the like, attempts to establish the method by which a book has been manufactured. Cf. *descriptive bibliography*. See **750–755**.

apocrypha A work formerly—and doubtfully or mistakenly—attributed to an author is said to belong to his apocrypha. *The Testament of Love* is in the Chaucer apocrypha (it actually is by Thomas Usk), and *Arden of Feversham* is in the Shakespeare apocrypha. Cf. *canon, corpus*.

ascription The conjecture, in the absence of definite proof, that a certain literary work was written by a given author. Thus *The Pricke of Conscience* once was, but no longer is, ascribed to Richard Rolle. Synonym: *attribution*.

147

association copy   A copy of a book once owned (or annotated) by
the author himself, or by someone otherwise associated with the
book, such as the prototype of a character, or by some famous
person.   For example, the Folger Library has thousands of association copies of Shakespeare, once owned and in some cases
annotated by people like Garrick, Johnson, Pope, Washington,
Coleridge, Lamb, Emerson, Lincoln, Shaw, and General Tom
Thumb.   For an interesting demonstration of the importance of
association copies in literary history and criticism, in this instance
Browning's first copy of Shelley's poems, see Frederick A. Pottle,
Shelley and Browning: A Myth and Some Facts (privately
printed, Chicago, 1923).

attribution   See *ascription, internal evidence.*

author bibliography   A list of works by—often also works about—
a certain author.   These bibliographies vary enormously in authority, scope, and detail, from bare unannotated *check lists*
(q.v.) to elaborate catalogues like Geoffrey Keynes's bibliography of John Donne (3rd ed., Cambridge, 1958) and Thomas J.
Holmes's bibliography of Cotton Mather (3 vols., Cambridge,
Mass., 1940).

bad quarto   A severely *corrupt* (q.v.) text of an Elizabethan play,
usually derived from the memory of an actor or playgoer.

bibliographical ghost   A book that has never existed.   Not to be
confused with a book that actually was published, but all copies
of which have disappeared.   See George Watson Cole, "Bibliographical Ghosts," *PBSA*, 13 (1919), 87–112.   There are also
biographical ghosts, like those which haunt *Appletons' Cyclopaedia* (**995**). In modern reference works, ghosts are sometimes
deliberately planted to forestall wholesale plagiarism; for example, in *Who's Who in America,* 30 (1958/9), the entry for
"Hansell, Samuel G." is fictitious.

black letter   The heavy-faced type, often called "gothic," or,
loosely, "Old English," in which many early books were printed.
Beginning in England in the late sixteenth century, black letter
was gradually replaced by roman (like this) and italic (*like this*).

calendar   A catalogue of manuscripts in a given collection, or by a
particular author irrespective of location; lists date, place, ad-

dressee (if any), number of leaves and other physical details, and often gives a summary of contents. For examples, see the Reports of the Historical Manuscripts Commission or the Calendars of State Papers (above, pages 121 and 125). Also used as a verb: "to make a calendar."

call-number　See *press-mark*.

cancel　A substitute leaf or pasted-in slip, inserted in a book after it is printed (and in most instances bound), to eliminate a serious error of fact, or a blasphemy, a libel, a political heresy, or some other indiscretion. Also used as a verb: "to delete the offending matter and insert the replacement." The standard treatise on the subject, with numerous interesting examples, is R. W. Chapman, *Cancels* (London, 1930).

canon　The total body of work accepted as by a certain author Cf. *corpus*.

case　See *font*.

catchword　The first word on a new page as it is anticipatorily printed in the lower right-hand corner of the preceding one. In old books, probably a device to help the printer arrange pages of type in the *forme* (q.v.).

chain-lines　In "laid" paper (which was used almost universally in books before the nineteenth century and is still found in some high-quality books), the widely spaced markings impressed into the paper by the wire mesh on which the pulp was set. Chain-lines are spaced about three-quarters to one inch apart. (The closer-set lines which run crosswise are called *wire-lines*.) Because chain-lines nearly always run parallel with the shorter dimension of the sheet to be folded, they are a valuable way of ascertaining the format of a book (running vertically in the leaf of a folio or an octavo, horizontally in a quarto). Not to be confused with *watermarks*.

check list　A bibliography, generally somewhat tentative, whose entries are in simple form, without technical elaboration.

codex　A manuscript volume; used especially of ancient and medieval texts. Plural: *codices*. Cf. *roll*.

collate   (1) To compare two versions of a text, or two copies of a book, word by word or line by line. In its oldest form, simply a process of looking from one book to another and noting variations; in its most refined and complicated modern form, a highly mechanized process which has resulted in, among other things, the discovery of several hundred hitherto unnoticed variants in the text of Shakespeare. See Charlton Hinman, "Mechanized Collation at the Houghton Library," *Harvard Library Bulletin*, 9 (1955), 132–34. (2) To analyze and describe the physical makeup of a book: format, number and designation of leaves, contents (dedication, preface, text, appendices, etc.), and presence of plates. For the best modern collation practices, see those followed in *Greg's* English Printed Drama (**412**).

colophon   In older books, a note at the end giving such information as author, title, printer, and sometimes date of issue: "Thus endeth thys noble and Ioyous book entytled le morte Darthur . . . whiche book was reduced iu to englysshe by syr Thomas Malory knyght as afore is sayd and by me deuyded in to xxi bookes chapytred and enprynted and fynyssed in thabbey westmestre the last day of Iuyl the yere of our lord mccccLxxxv Caxton me fieri fecit." In modern books, the term is sometimes used for the publisher's house-emblem or device: e.g., the Knopf borzoi, the Viking ship, the Holt owl, the Harper and Row torch.

conflation   A merging of variant tests into one. The editor assumes the responsibility of deciding which of the alternate readings are the closest to the author's intentions, and thus the readings to be adopted into what is, at best, an artificial reconstruction. A conflated text (sometimes called *eclectic*) has the same purpose as a *critical text*.

copy text   The text of a work, in print or in manuscript, from which a new edition is set. More narrowly, the edition or manuscript which is closest to the author's intention and which is used as the basis for a critical edition. A classic discussion is W. W. Greg, "The Rationale of Copy Text," *Studies in Bibliography*, 3 (1950/51), 19–36. See *critical text*.

corpus   The whole body of writings by a given author (in this sense the same as *canon*), or on a given subject.

corrupt Inaccurate, unfaithful to the original; used of any faulty literary text. See *bad quarto, critical text*.

critical bibiliography A list of books with descriptive and evaluative annotations.

critical text (or **edition**) An authoritatively edited text of a work, usually based on the readings in the original manuscript, or the first edition, or the last edition corrected by the author. The critical text of a medieval work is based on a collation of manuscripts and the establishment of the best manuscript tradition, families of manuscripts, etc. In establishing a critical text— whether of a medieval or a modern work—the primary aim is to eliminate the corruptions (that is, the errors and gratuitous emendations) that have crept into the text since it left the hands of the author. The Manly and Rickert edition of *The Canterbury Tales* is critical in this sense; critical texts of Keats's poems have been made by Ernest de Selincourt and by H. W. Garrod. Cf. *conflation, recension, variorum edition.*

crux A word or passage in a text that is puzzling or does not seem to make sense; often blamed on careless typesetting or misreading of difficult handwriting. In many editions of Shakespeare, cruxes are marked by a cross-like dagger (†). Cf. *emendation.*

descriptive bibliography The branch of scholarship which, by analyzing and recording a book's title page, format, pagination, etc., can determine variant *editions, impressions,* and *issues* (qq.v.). Cf. *analytical bibliography.*

device A decoration, such as a shop-sign, crest, coat of arms, or emblem, which appears on the title page or final leaf of a book and identifies the book as the work of a certain printer or publisher. The precise state of a device in a given book—degree of wear, presence of small variations in the design, etc.—often affords a valuable clue to the date of printing. The standard guide is R. B. McKerrow, *Printers' and Publishers' Devices in England and Scotland, 1485–1640* (London, 1913). Cf. *colophon.*

diplomatic text A text which reproduces that of a manuscript as exactly as possible within the limitations of typography, including all irregularities of spelling and punctuation, mistakes, and corrections.

document Any piece of manuscript (and, in the broadest usage, printed material as well) that contains information. Personal letters, diaries, legal papers, newspaper clippings, university records, laundry lists—all are documents. The collection of pamphlets and letters called "The Old Yellow Book" is the chief documentary source of Browning's *The Ring and the Book.*

duodecimo A book made up of sheets folded into twelve leaves. This is more familiarly referred to as *twelvemo* and is abbreviated *12mo.*

eclectic text see *conflation.*

edition This is a term that has been, and is, very loosely used. In general, it designates all the copies of a book that are printed from one setting of type; the various printings may be spaced over months or years. A new edition is produced only when substantial changes have been made in the text (beyond a certain amount of minor revision), or when the type has been entirely reset. Cf. *impression, issue.*

emendation An editor's correction of a reading in a text, to restore what he knows, or has reason to think, the author really meant to say. The most famous emendation in English literary history is the editor Theobald's alteration of Dame Quickly's description of the dying Falstaff in *Henry V* (II.iii.17)—"and a Table of greene fields"—to "and a babbled of green fields." Cf. *variant* (*reading*).

external evidence Any evidence, apart from that found in the text itself, bearing upon authorship, date and circumstances of composition, sources, etc. of a literary work. Such evidence may consist of historical or biographical facts, or may be produced by physical analysis of manuscripts or by study of printing practices, papers, inks, bindings, and the like. Cf. *internal evidence.* The most celebrated modern example of the use of both external and internal evidence, in this case to test the authenticity of literary documents suspected of being forgeries, is John Carter and

Graham Pollard, *An Enquiry into the Nature of Certain Nineteenth Century Pamphlets* (New York, 1934).

extra-illustrated See *grangerized.*

fascicle A separately assembled and sometimes separately issued part of a book. Blake's *Illustrations of the Book of Job,* edited by Laurence Binyon and Geoffrey Keynes (New York, 1935), is made up of unbound fascicles of several versions of the Job designs.

foliation The numbering of a book's constituent parts by leaves rather than by pages: in printed books, a practice abandoned about 1600, but still retained in manuscript volumes.

folio (1) A large book made up of sheets folded only once. (2) The leaf of a manuscript or book (used chiefly of books lacking pagination). Abbreviated *f.* or *fol.* (plural: *ff.* or *fols.*).

font (British spelling: *fount*) In a printing house, a complete assortment of type of one style and size. For hand setting, each font is kept in a pair of shallow compartmented trays, called *cases.* The capital letters of type are kept in the upper tray and so are referred to as *upper case;* the small letters are kept in the lower tray and so are referred to as *lower case.* For specimens of various type faces see the University of Chicago Press *Manual of Style* (33).

format In bibliographical terminology, the physical makeup of a book as determined by the number of times each sheet has been folded (folio, quarto, octavo, etc.). In popular modern usage, all the physical features of a book, including the style of typography and binding. Note that in older library usage, and in current bookselling terminology, the terms *folio, quarto,* etc. designate the size of a book without relation to the number of times its sheets have been folded to make leaves. While it is true that a folio is the largest book, a quarto the next largest, and so on down to a virtually invisible 128°, these terms are only rough approximations, since there is wide variation in the size of the *sheet* (q.v.). Hence the scientific bibliographer never uses them to refer to size except, perhaps, when talking with a bookseller.

forme A body of type laid out in a printer's *chase* or frame, comprising all the pages that will be printed on one side of a single sheet (in hand printing, two pages for a folio, four for a quarto, and so on). When the printed sheet is turned over and an equivalent number of pages printed on the blank side from another forme, it is said to be *perfected*.

front matter Everything preceding the main text of a book—title page, dedication, table of contents, foreword, preface, etc. Also called the *preliminaries* or, more informally, the *prelims*.

galley A long shallow tray in which composed type—about three pages' worth—is kept until it is divided into pages. From the standing type in this unpaged state *galley proofs* are "pulled."

gathering One section of a book, composed of the leaves into which a single sheet has been folded. In the case of a folio and occasionally of a quarto, more than one sheet—sometimes, also, half a sheet—is included. Approximate synonyms: *quire, signature* (sense 1).

ghost See *bibliographical ghost*.

grangerized Describes a copy of a book which has been "enriched" and often monstrously enlarged by the insertion of illustrations, autograph letters, and other material more or less related to the subject of the book. The term derives from James Granger, who published in 1769 a history of England, "with blank leaves for engraved portraits, etc." Boswell's *Life of Johnson* has often been thus treated; so also have histories of New England, topographical works, studies of Regency society, and other books of this sort. Synonym: *extra-illustrated*.

historical bibliography The historical study of papermaking, typefounding, illustration, printing, binding, publishing, bookselling, and allied arts and trades: the history of the book as a manufactured object and as an article of commerce. Cf. **750–780.**

holograph A manuscript wholly in the handwriting of its author. The word is also used as an adjective.

illumination The art, which reached its height in the middle ages, of decorating and illustrating manuscripts, particularly their initial letters and margins.

impression All copies of a book produced by a run of sheets through the press at one time. Involves no fresh setting of type and therefore not to be called an *edition* (q.v.); an edition may consist of several impressions. Synonym: *printing*. Cf. *issue*.

imprint Publishing information (specifically, the name of the publisher or, in the case of old books, the printer, accompanied by place of publication, and, usually, date) found at the bottom of the title page. Cf. *colophon*.

incipit The first line, especially of a medieval text; used to designate the text because there is no distinctive title. "Somer is comen wiþ loue to toune" is the first line, or incipit, of a poem in MS. Bodley 1687, f. 186ᵇ. "Indexes to first lines" in modern collections of poems are indexes to incipits.

incunabula (plural) Books printed before the year 1501. Singular forms: *incunabulum, incunable* (plural: *incunables*).

inscribed copy See *presentation copy*.

internal evidence The evidence produced by an analysis of a given text which throws light on its authorship, date, circumstances of composition, etc. Habits of literary style, imagery, and allusions to contemporary events are familiar kinds of internal evidence. Cf. *external evidence*. For a comprehensive discussion, see *Evidence for Authorship*, ed. David V. Erdman and Ephim G. Fogel (Ithaca, 1966), and for specific applications in a limited field, S. Schoenbaum, *Internal Evidence and Elizabethan Authorship: An Essay in Literary History and Method* (Evanston, 1966).

issue Those copies of an impression which differ from others of the same impression in that changes have been made after publication—chiefly those which alter some of the details of publication and sale, i.e., the title page and other preliminaries. Cf. *cancel, edition, impression*.

leaf The smallest physical unit of a book, either side of which is a page. Thus the basic bibliographical equation: one leaf equals two pages.

lower case See *font*.

microform, microtext   Inclusive terms for all processes by which
books and manuscripts are reproduced in very small scale for
reading through special machines.   *Microfilm,* the oldest and
most common process, involves the use of (generally) 35 mm.
film, on each frame of which a single page or two-page opening
is reproduced.   A *microfiche* is a sheet of microfilm in card form
of various sizes containing a number of separate positive or nega-
tive images.   A *microprint,* also in card form (usually 6 x 9
inches), is printed from a plate containing about one hundred
pages, photographically reduced from an ordinary book.   Im-
mense quantities of research materials are now available in one
or another of these forms; see, for example, entries for *STC*
(**795**) and Evans (**822**); the *Guide to Microforms in Print*
(**830**) and the *National Register of Microform Masters* (**831**).

national bibliography   A list of all books issued in a given country
irrespective of author or subject.

octavo   A book made up of sheets each of which has been folded
three times to make eight leaves.   Abbreviated *8vo* or *8°*.

offprint   A copy of an article printed from the type used for its
prior appearance in a journal or a book of multiple authorship.
Distributing offprints or *separates* of one's published works to
colleagues and fellow-specialists is a hallowed scholarly ritual.

O.P.   "Out of print"; describes a book no longer available from the
publisher.   Differs from "out of stock," which implies that the
shortage is temporary and that a new supply will be obtained
from the printer.

page proof   Proof pulled from standing type after it has been divided into pages.   Cf. *galley.*   Ordinarily the last chance the
author has to make corrections before his work goes to press.

paleography   The study of old handwriting, down to about the
seventeenth century.

parchment   The predecessor of paper, usually made from the skin
of sheep or goats.   Cf. *vellum.*

presentation copy   A copy of a book that its author gave to someone else, as proved, usually, by an inscription in his own hand.

An *inscribed copy*, on the contrary, bears no proof of being a gift; it may just as well have been purchased by the owner and signed by the author ("With best wishes, Norman Mailer") at a department-store autographing party.

press-mark The letters and numbers that indicate a book's place on the library shelves. Synonym: *shelf-mark*. Both are British usage. American equivalent: *call-number*.

primary source Documentary testimony of the central figures, witnesses, or first recorders of an event; e.g., a contemporary chronicle, diary, or newspaper account. Cf. *secondary source*.

printing Synonymous with *impression*, q.v.

provenance The history of a particular volume or manuscript, especially the record of its successive owners. John Carter speaks of a fictitious volume known as "The Coningsby-Locksley Hall-Hentzau-Casamassima-D'Urberville copy." For aids in tracing provenance, see **727–744**.

quarto A book made up of sheets each of which has been folded twice to make four leaves. Abbreviated *4to* or *4°* or *Q*.

quire See *gathering*.

recension This somewhat loosely used term, roughly equivalent to *version*, designates a re-working of a literary text by someone other than the author, with the implication of thorough revision rather than of incidental touching-up. Used especially, but not exclusively, in connection with Biblical and medieval texts.

recto The right-hand page of an open book. Hence "leaf A4ʳ" refers to the front of the fourth leaf in a gathering, or the seventh page. The page you are looking at is a recto. Cf. *verso*.

roll A document which, following medieval English filing practice, was preserved by being rolled up rather than by being included in a volume (cf. *codex*). In the case of parchment membranes rolled up individually, *roll* is synonymous with *scroll;* more usually, however, particularly in government offices, membranes were sewn together end to end, forming rolls thirty or forty feet long when laid flat.

rubric   A note or heading in a manuscript, often in red (hence the name), giving information about the author, scribe, date or title, or any combination thereof.   Medieval manuscripts did not have title pages; the rubric is the ancestor of the title page.   The *colophon* (q.v.) was sometimes used as the concluding rubric.

running title   The short title of a book or chapter which appears at the top of each normal page (such as this one).   By tracing the recurrence of each set of running titles, a bibliographer often learns how the book was printed, whether there were interruptions in the process, how many presses were used, and even the number of compositors.

scribal error   A mistake in a manuscript attributed to the copyist, or *scribe*.

secondary source   Documentary or other evidence which is not first-hand.   Generally, a book, article, or other work which incorporates or purports to incorporate evidence found in *primary sources* (q.v.).   John Stuart Mill's *Autobiography* (1874) is a primary source, Michael St. John Packe's *The Life of John Stuart Mill* (1954) is a secondary source.

serial   In library usage, any work whose successive parts are issued at intervals, without any expectation of an end.   The range is from weekly magazines to scholarly journals, reports of corporations, and the annals of learned societies.   *The Year's Work in English Studies* (**454**), the *Bibliographic Index* (**504**), *PMLA* (**630**), and *Dissertation Abstracts International* (**837**) are all serials.   But the Yale edition of the letters of Horace Walpole, which will eventually be completed, is not.

sheet   The rectangular piece of paper that serves as a unit in book printing.   The size was never standardized, but in Shakespeare's time, for instance, two very common sizes were 15 x 20 inches and 12 x 16 inches.   Folded once, such a sheet provided two leaves or four pages (folio); folded twice, four leaves or eight pages (quarto); folded three times, eight leaves or sixteen pages (octavo), and so on.   Much larger sheets are used in modern printing.   This book was printed on sheets measuring 45 x 68 inches, 64 pages to a *forme,* q.v.

shelf-mark   See *press-mark*.

signature   (1) A printed sheet folded to constitute a unit of a book. Either alone or, in folios and some quartos, folded with one to three other sheets, equivalent to a *gathering* or *quire*. (2) The printer's mark, a letter, number, or symbol, which appears at the bottom of the recto of at least the first leaf of a sheet as folded. It guides the binder in assembling the folded gatherings in the right sequence (and the bibliographer in collating the book). Signatures in this latter sense are still regularly found in British books but seldom in modern books printed in the United States.

sixteenmo   A book made up of sheets each of which has been folded into sixteen leaves. The common substitute for *sexto-decimo;* abbreviated *16mo* or *16°*.

state   A term used to differentiate variant copies of a book produced during a single press run and before the book has been offered for sale. Thus any textual changes during one pre-publication printing result in two or more states. To be differentiated from *issue*, q.v.

stationer   The older term for a tradesman who published or sold books, or both (stationers also had many sidelines). A stationer might also be a printer, but often was not. Beginning in the sixteenth century the trade divided itself into printers, publishers, and retail booksellers; by the nineteenth century the word *stationer* came to refer almost exclusively to dealers in writing materials.

subject bibliography   A list of books (and sometimes articles) about any subject. Relation to *author bibliography:* a list solely of books *about* a given author could be called a subject bibliography, but if it were added to one containing works *by* the author, the total product would be classified as an author bibliography.

substantives   See *accidentals*.

textual criticism   The branch of scholarship dedicated to examining critically the text(s) of a literary work, with the ultimate goal of determining as accurately as possible their origin, or their history, or what the author really wrote. Now closely connected with some phases of *analytical bibliography* (q.v.). See **863–867**. Cf. *critical text, recension.*

twelvemo See *duodecimo.*

uncut Describes a book the edges of whose leaves, though "opened," have not been trimmed down by the binder. Not to be confused with *unopened* (q.v.).

unique copy The only copy of a certain book that is known to exist.

universal bibliography A list of books with no limitations of subject, author, or time or place of origin.

unopened Describes a book whose leaves remain folded (closed) just as they were when the binder put together the component folded sheets. They have not been "opened" by the binder's shears or the reader's knife. A book that is *uncut* can be read; a book that is *unopened* cannot.

upper case See *font.*

variant (reading) One of two or more different versions of a given word or passage in a work. Where one version is, for one reason or another, accepted as standard, the other version is often called the variant; but the term can be applied equally to either version. In *Hamlet,* I.ii.129, the Folio reads "O that this too too solid flesh would melt," while the First and Second Quartos read *sallied.* Or should it be emended to *sullied?* The controversy has raged ever since J. Dover Wilson argued for *sullied* (*What Happens in Hamlet,* Cambridge, 1935). An attractive variant reading in the General Prologue to *The Canterbury Tales* (line 386), adopted by two fifteenth-century scribes but not by fastidious modern editors, would place the Cook's running "mormal" where it belongs for maximum effect: not on his *shyne* but on his *chynne.*

variorum edition An edition of a single literary work, or the collected works of an author, which contains a comprehensive collection of annotation and commentary by previous scholars. The term is also now used for an edition which attempts systematically to list all variant readings, both those found in contemporary manuscripts and editions and those proposed as emendations by later editors. Recent examples of variorums, in the latter sense, are editions of Yeats by Peter Allt and Russell K. Alspach (New York, 1957) and of Emily Dickinson by T. H. Johnson (Cambridge, Mass., 1955). The most famous example in English literature of a variorum which contains both textual variants and a copious selection of earlier commentary is the still unfinished *New Variorum Shakespeare*.

vellum   A fine grade of parchment made of calfskin.

verso   The left-hand page of an open book. The page facing this is a verso. See *recto*.

watermark   The paper maker's trademark, sometimes a crude pictorial design, at other times one or more initials or words or a date, impressed into paper by twisted or soldered wires set into the screen on which the pulp sets (cf. *chain-lines*). An important means by which scholars can approximately date, and sometimes establish the place of origin of, a book that is otherwise unidentified. See **756**. Also useful in helping to ascertain the format of a book. Until the end of the eighteenth century, the watermark was regularly placed in the center of one half of the sheet (as divided parallel with the shorter dimension). Thus the place where it appears in a gathering offers a clue as to how many times the sheet was folded.

wire-lines   See *chain-lines*.

Index

Except where indicated, references in the text
are to numbered items rather than to pages.

NY Times Biographical Ed